THE
FAIRY GODMOTHER'S
GROWTH GUIDE

*Whimsical Poems and
Radical Prose
for Self-Exploration*

MARISA McGRADY

ViVa
EDITIONS

Published in the United States by Viva Editions, an imprint of Start Midnight, LLC, 221 River Street, Ninth Floor, Hoboken, New Jersey 07030.
Printed in the United States

Cover design: Jennifer Do
Cover image: Shutterstock/FIDAN.STOCK, LaInspiratriz, lucky strokes
Text design: Frank Wiedemann

First Edition.
10 9 8 7 6 5 4 3 2 1

Trade paper ISBN: 978-1-63228-088-6
E-book ISBN: 978-1-63228-145-6

To you, my dear.

You are the reason I'm here.

Contents

CONTENTS

CONTENTS

DISCLAIMER

The suggestions and recommendations made in this book are based on the author's knowledge, experience, and opinions. The methods described in this book are not intended to be a definitive set of instructions. Other methods and materials may accomplish the same end results. Results may vary. There are no representations or warranties, express or implied, about the completeness, accuracy, or reliability of the information, products, services, or related materials contained in this book. The information is provided as is, to be used at your own risk.

This book is not intended as a substitute for consultation with a licensed health-care practitioner, such as your physician. Before you begin any health-care program or make lifestyle changes in any way, please consult a physician or another licensed health-care practitioner to ensure that the examples contained in this book will not cause any harm. If you or someone you know is suffering from addiction, depression/other mental health issues, eating disorders, or the like, please seek initial medical attention. Where appropriate, identities have been obscured out of concern for privacy.

PREFACE

W hat makes a body good or bad?
Is it the same thing that makes a person good or bad?
Are good and bad the only options?
Can we be something else, something in between?
Who decides?
Ultimately, my dear, you do. Don't fret. That's a *good* thing.

These questions pained me when I was younger. I wanted someone else to give me the answers, preferably in a nice, neat, bulleted list. I wished a fairy godmother would wave their magic wand and "*poof!*" my pain into peace, but *apparently* that's not how it works. We decide for ourselves. We all find and create our own answers to life's big questions, and those answers evolve as we evolve.

It's tough to make sense of your mind, your body, and the

world around you when everything constantly changes. Plans change. People change. Places change. Just when you finally figure yourself and your life out, *you* change. The known reverts to the unknown. The unknown expands, and *"BOOM!"* you start over again at square one. That's a lot to handle for us humble humans, as powerful and magical as we are. If it's any consolation, I believe we prove our progress, not erase it, when we start over. Each time we go back to square one, we go back with more knowledge, experience, and perspective. We learn or realize something new each time we try, regardless of the outcome.

If you're anything like me, you may not find that concept comforting right now. Perhaps you want a fairy godmother to *"poof!"* your problems away, too. If so, today's your lucky day.

I can be your fairy godmother, if you'll have me. I can wave my magic wand and clarify the chaos flying around about self-love, self-care, and those ever-intriguing, ever-irritating existential questions. I can make you a nice, neat, bulleted list of suggestions and advice based on my lived experience—a fairy godmother's growth guide, if you will—and you can decide whether or not it resonates with you. I cannot answer the big questions *for* you, my dear, but I can work *with* you to help you find and create your own answers. We can work together to make life more magical.

I won't sugarcoat things. I won't shy away from tough topics. I won't ask you to be anything or anyone other than you. You don't have to earn my love or support—you already have it. Just say the magic word,[1] and we can begin.

Splendid! All right, we've got a lot to cover. Let's start with the basics.

---

1 Pick whichever word you like. Any word can be magical if you intend it to be. That said, if you pick a word that might get you in trouble, perhaps you should whisper it under your breath instead of saying it out loud.

Have you heard those cheesy sayings about life, being yourself, and trying your best?

"You know yourself best!"
"Your best is enough!"
"Progress over perfection!"

They're all true. Cliché, overused, and misused at times, but true.

Before you roll your eyes at me, I get it. I rolled my eyes at these sayings and the people who parroted them for twenty years. Well-intended folks often smushed these sentiments in with other, lesser sayings, like "Look for the silver lining."

Ick!

That saying irks me. I don't know about you, but I didn't want to be told to look for a silver lining while my life unraveled around me. I wanted help. I wanted guidance. I wanted a genuinely empathetic response.

Sometimes life sucks. It's okay to admit that. Even the most magical, positive beings face difficult days, weeks, months, and years. Yes, life can be beautiful, inspiring, and fun. It can also be painful, unpredictable, and exhausting. Acknowledging this duality does not make someone a pessimist. Perspective is a powerful tool, but it cannot replace our need to feel and express human emotions. Everyone grapples with grief, sorrow, and anger eventually. Even if all situations technically contain some kind of silver lining, forcing positivity into moments of active, genuine pain denies us part of our humanity, prevents us from regulating and processing pain, and takes optimism to an unhealthy extreme. Perhaps sayings about silver linings inherently include this subtext. I took most things literally as a teenager.[2] Since the subtext wasn't spelled out, I found sayings about silver linings reductive and, frankly, ridiculous.

My anger grew each time I sought support only to be met with superficial niceties that dismissed my pain at best and invalidated it at worst. My heart shrank a size smaller with each new disappointment. When death, instability, and dysfunctional dynamics ravaged my life, I bristled at the mere *thought* of someone telling me to focus on the good. I wished I could. I knew things could be worse. Guilt gnawed at me every time someone scolded me for lacking gratitude. I appreciated the roof over my head, but I feared what occurred beneath it. Every day, I stared up at the roof as the walls caught fire. Smoke filled my lungs. Hot ash scorched my skin. I willed myself to focus on the good while everything around me burned,[3] and I blamed myself when I failed to find silver linings amid the wreckage.

As I grew older, the raging, wrathful flames within me dulled to controlled, cranky coals. The heat and hurt still simmered, but I was exhausted. Apathy crept in. My teenage self didn't understand how or why the adults with all the freedom to live their lives autonomously wouldn't teach me how to live mine. I didn't understand why authority figures who had the power to police my behavior wouldn't tell me how to process my emotions so I could behave according to their expectations—responsibly, quietly, and peacefully.[4] I didn't want to be overwhelmed by fear, rage, and

---

2   I still take most things literally, which is funny considering how much I adore fantasy, magic, and make-believe. Most humans are walking contradictions. I'm no exception.

3   Remember when I said I take most things literally, but I'm also guilty of contradictions? The last four sentences of this paragraph serve to demonstrate past instability and pain in my life. My house was not literally on fire.

4   Who gave them that power, anyway? If I had a dollar for every time I sincerely asked an adult why I should do what they told me to do and they responded with "Because I said so," I'd have enough dollars to pay for therapy.

despair. Nobody does. I didn't want to get in trouble. I was a Goody-Two-shoes with anxiety. Getting in trouble vexed me. I had exceptional grades, led and excelled in extracurriculars, respected my curfews, kept in constant communication with the adults in my life, worked multiple jobs, and didn't dabble in illegal activities. I wanted what the adults wanted—to be trusted to be left alone—so it agitated me to my core that they faulted me for things like my tone and disposition no matter how well I followed the rules. Even if I said and did all the right things, they didn't like *how* I said and did them. It felt so unfair. Like an "I'm going to stomp my sparkly silver shoes into the fairy forest floor, snap my magic wand over my knee, and shout, 'Are you kidding me?!' up at the stars" level of unfairness.

I resented most people who tried to help almost as much as I resented people who didn't. I found their advice insufficient. Each time someone coughed up strained sayings about silver linings in an attempt to console me, I withdrew deeper into avoidance and annoyance. I interpreted superficial support as a sign that adults didn't consider me worth their time and teachings. I worried I'd done something bad—or maybe not done enough good—to deserve their dismissal. I couldn't figure out what to do differently. I felt certain that the adults living and working in the real world knew how to self-regulate. Surely they knew how to handle things like death, grief, and fear of the unknown, so why wouldn't they teach me how to do the same? I didn't realize the adults might not have all the answers, either.

We rely on information to make decisions and interact with others. Sometimes we act instantly on gut feelings. Sometimes we ruminate over all the possible paths forward for what feels like an eternity. In either instance, we often blame people—ourselves and others—for undesirable outcomes. We convince ourselves that we have all the information we need to get things right, and we grow angry, frustrated, sad, and confused when things go wrong. But we don't know what we don't know. We don't know the limitations and truth of what we do know. People are only ever partially to blame.

Sometimes the issue lies with the available information.

When we base our decisions on faulty or incomplete information, we can get undesired outcomes. The subjectivity of human perception and the relativity of the human experience complicate information's reliability. For example, let's say Person A swears that drinking herbal tea is life-changing. Person A could be telling the truth, but that information might not help Person B because the "life-changing" impact of drinking herbal tea may only be true relative to the conditions of Person A's existence. Person A's lifestyle, body, and personal taste make herbal tea life-changing for them, but Person B has their own unique lifestyle, body, and personal taste. Therefore, Person A's assessment that "drinking herbal tea is life-changing" can be both true and untrue at the same time, because it's based on subjective conditions. This may seem obvious in this context, but you'd be surprised how often humans (me included) conflate subjective truths and objective truths and experience distress as a result.

Person A didn't lie. Person A didn't do anything wrong. If we specified the exact nature and conditions for every piece of information we share and clarified the objectiveness or subjectiveness of its truth every time we shared it, our conversations would quickly convolute. Anyone in this hypothetical example who decides to drink herbal tea based on Person A's experience might not get the outcome they desire, but that isn't Person A's or anyone else's fault. The issue would be the **relative, subjective truth** of Person A's lived experience and the **incomplete nature of the information shared.**

We learn how to live based on what we know. Sometimes we're unaware that what we know is inaccurate, incomplete, subjective, or relative. We can't beat ourselves up for the outcomes of our choices without examining the information that informed our choices.[5] The same idea applies to self-love. Self-love, self-care, and self-worth are all subjective, relative concepts. Anyone who claims that they can teach you about these concepts (and consequently about yourself) without acknowledging the subjective, relative, and limited nature of their information should not be trusted.

There is no singular objective truth about how to love and care for yourself. There is no right or wrong way to be you. Any guidance, steps, instructions, opinions, advice, or information offered about concepts like self-love is always limited, at least in part, by the lived experience and knowledge of the person offering it. No one knows you as well as you do. No matter how well someone knows or claims to know you, the secondary data they collect and possess about you by observing you can't contend with the data you collect and possess by living as you. This is where the first of those cheesy sayings comes into play.

"You know yourself best."

You know your needs.
You know your wants.
You know your fears.

---

5 I'm not saying get rid of accountability. We all make mistakes. To err is human. When we mess up, we should hold ourselves accountable and do our best not to repeat harmful behaviors (whether we intended harm or not). However, if we try to do something with good intentions, and we still get unwanted or harmful outcomes, we ought to examine the information that informed our actions *after* we take accountability for them but *before* we use them to justify self-hatred.

You know even the unknowable, unconscious parts of yourself more than anyone else ever can.

If you're shaking your head at me and saying, "But I don't know what I need. I barely know how to survive. I barely know what I did last Tuesday! I want someone to tell me how to do this. How do I love and care for myself? How do I deal with pain? *How do I live?*"

I see you. I crave objective answers and instructions, too. I know it might seem frightening, overwhelming, unreasonable, or even impossible to trust yourself, especially if someone or something has convinced you that your understanding of reality can't be trusted, but **you *do* know yourself best**. Therefore, you are the most qualified person to teach yourself how to live. I and many others can help you. We can offer you information and guidance, but you must teach yourself. You decide whether our information interests you. You consider and evaluate new perspectives, compare them to alternative perspectives, and decide which ones feel right for you. You practice new behaviors and determine what they can and can't provide for you. You've already been doing all this and living your life successfully up until today, whether you think so or not. Forget about external measures of success. You're here.

You're alive.

No matter who or what helped you, you sustained your life until this very moment. You continue to sustain your life with each passing word you read. You, my dear, are maintaining your life right now, no matter how well or poorly you think you're doing it. While you were begging, searching, or waiting for someone to tell you how to live, you were already living, even if it's not exactly how you want to be living yet.

The wonderful, magical thing about that is that we can change how we live at any moment. Structural and individual barriers make certain kinds of change challenging or difficult to access,[6] but we can still exercise autonomy within those limitations in small but meaningful ways. We can try something new. We can retry something old. You picked up this book, for example. That was you trying something new. Maybe you went back to an old routine or preference recently after experimenting with a new one. You tried something new, evaluated how you liked it, and decided you preferred your original choice. You trusted yourself. You changed your mind. You exercised your autonomy. Only you know all the tiny details, actions, and thought processes that go into these seemingly mundane daily exercises of autonomy. You have the most accurate, comprehensive understanding of yourself and what it's like to live your life.

You are the only qualified expert on you. You know yourself best, and we know that information impacts our decisions. As your fairy godmother, it's my solemnly sworn duty to provide the best supplemental information I can to help you decide how you want to live your life each day. It's not your fault if all the cheesy, optimistic ideas about life, growth, and self-love annoy you. They annoyed me, too, because they're incomplete. They're relative, subjective, and open to interpretation. No one ever explained the exact nature, conditions, applications of, and contradictions between these ideas to me. They certainly didn't expand on the implications and limitations of these ideas in the wider world, but I will do my darnedest to explain all these things to you based on my understanding of them.

Let me emphasize the *my* in the previous sentence. "My" as in "relative to me." My understanding and information are limited.

---

6   And we will address that in this book. Self-worth is not just an internal concept. It's impacted by our external world and consequently by the world's injustices.

My stories and examples are based on my lived experience, though I do my best to provide objective definitions for terms to make this text more cohesive and digestible. You decide whether my opinions, interpretations, and perspectives benefit you or not. I can advocate for why I think my ideas deserve consideration, but I can't decide whether you consider them. Only you can do that.

I cannot be you.[7]

I cannot tell you exactly how to live your life, how to love and care for yourself, or what will work best for you specifically. Only you can assess and do that.

I can be your fairy godmother. I can share all my poems and perspectives to help empower and inform you. I can offer you genuine empathy and share my stories about pain and growth so you know you aren't alone. I can tell you how I care for myself without judgment or expectation and how it helps me. I can tell you why self-care can't solve everything. I can tell you about the ways I messed up, what I learned from the experiences, and what I do differently now.

I can show you how I make life magical for myself, but you must make your life magical. Other people, places, experiences, and resources can and will add to your magic, but only you can create and protect it.

Only you can live your life.

And you are the most qualified, capable person to do so.

I *pinkie* promise.

---

7   And I don't need to be. You're already doing a lovely job being you, my dear, and I'm busy being me.

INTRODUCTION

L ife has inherent light. This light goes by many names. Some people call it a soul. Some people call it the self. Some people call it consciousness or energy. Whatever we call it, we collectively understand that it is the intangible, inherent *something* that distinguishes life from nonlife. I call it "light."

What you call this intangible, inherent something and how you prove, disprove, or define it is up to you. Your beliefs about life are your business. Your quality of life is my business. You made it my business when you opened this book, said the magic word, and made me your fairy godmother.[8]

I cannot tell you exactly how to live your life or why we're all here. Only you can answer those big questions for yourself. I

---

8   If you read the preface, that is. If you didn't, don't worry. I'm still here and happy to help.

can and will share my story and all I've learned about building sustainable, accommodating self-care practices and resilient self-worth. I hope to help you learn from my mistakes.

I also hope to help lighten your heart. Before my tenure as a fairy godmother, I was a stuffy, sad person who thought art had to be serious or solemn to be valuable. What a bunch of phooey! Much like magic, art is what we make and believe it to be. I wrote rhyming poems to uplift and entertain you. Read them with silly voices and rambunctious rhythms. I penned prose to empower you and expose you to new perspectives, and I sprinkled it with footnotes full of fairy dust.

Whether you read any of it or not is none of my business. You have my support either way. Do what feels right for you. I want you to trust yourself enough to decide what "right" means and to act on it, both in this context and throughout life. You can ask other people for input, but you determine whether something aligns with you and your values. I want you to love yourself enough to know you can change your mind and make mistakes, too. Being wrong about something is not a moral failing. You're always free to learn and try again.

There is no one-size-fits-all way to live life. We do our best to figure it out as we go. We learn, apply, and repeat. We tweak things until they work. We try new things, meet new people, and explore new places. Our beliefs evolve and solidify as we grow. We know that religion, spirituality, philosophy, and certain sciences carry different weight for different people. We recognize that what works for us may not make sense to someone else. We respect each other's autonomy because we know the struggle intimately. It's hard to understand yourself, especially when you're still trying to understand everything else. *GALAXIES . . . ? GOD(S) . . . ? FAMILY . . . ? PLEASURE . . . ? PAIN . . . ?*

It's a *lot* to take in all at once.

No one asked us if we wanted to be born. At least, not that we can remember. As far as we know, we just showed up one day, and we've all been trying to figure life out ever since. We know this about ourselves and each other. We get it. There are exceptions, unfortunately, but for the most part, we see each other human to human. Person to person. We acknowledge each other and say, "I'm doing my best, you're doing your best, and that's all there is," and we offer each other compassion within that. We make sense of our lives as we live them. We have to. It's all we can do.

Why, then, is it not the same for self-love? Where did mainstream ideas and expectations about self-love come from, and why are so many of them superficial, unsustainable, and inaccessible? Why are genuine insecurities and negative emotions feared, shamed, and dismissed? How can anyone advocate for self-love without addressing self-hatred and its roots? How do multibillion-dollar-budget "wellness" and self-help industries manage to make us feel worse? Who benefits—or more so, *profits*—from that?

Modern media oversimplifies self-love. The most freely, instantly accessible resources dominate and dictate popular narratives about our internal selves. These resources primarily exist online. Mass digital media outlets, social media influencers, and other online thought leaders often use *self-love* as a blanket term for a variety of concepts with differing definitions (like self-worth, self-esteem, and self-acceptance). They describe self-love as an emotion or positive feeling rather than as an awareness of yourself and your needs. They say you can achieve these loving feelings for yourself by treating yourself—buying your favorite flowers and chocolates, for example—without explaining that these singular acts of self-care do not serve the same purpose as sustainable self-care practices designed to help you meet your basic needs.

Feelings fade and fluctuate. Temporary happiness derived from singular acts of self-care cannot create durable self-worth.

Popular self-love narratives often leave these details out in favor of generalizations and toxic positivity.[9] These generalizations and toxic positivity, however well or ill intended, can hurt and confuse people more than they help them. They hurt and confused *me* for over a decade. I hated myself for "failing" at self-love before I realized I wasn't the problem. The problem, which I will do my best to rectify for you in this book, was inaccurate and incomplete information.

OUR FIRST THOUGHTS

Self-love did not come naturally to me. Some folks talked about it when I was younger. No one modeled it. The most influential people around me deprecated, doubted, and/or neglected themselves. Many of them didn't know any better. They weren't taught how to care for and love themselves, either. They cautioned me against following in their footsteps but never took their own advice. They muttered, "Do as I say, not as I do," and forgot that children learn by imitation. Thus, the cycle continued. I listened to what they said but observed what they did. I studied how they treated themselves, internalized how they treated me, and pondered the juxtaposition between their public and private behaviors. I watched. I listened. I mimicked and learned.

I grew up in the suburbs of a small, southern city in America during the early 2000s. Local and national pop culture reinforced the behaviors and mind-sets I observed around me. The ideal southern, Christian woman ought to be slender and deli-

---

9   Toxic positivity is a flawed approach to emotional regulation that encourages people to ignore, suppress, or hide negative emotions. We'll chat more about this in Chapters 2 and 3.

cate. Little girls should be "seen, not heard." Tabloids and magazine covers that compared "best and worst beach bodies" lined every grocery store checkout aisle. Talk show hosts wailed about weight gain and whispered about weight loss in the same breath. Hatred haunted every hall: at home, at school, at church, at the mall. I couldn't escape it, and as a tall, curvy, mentally ill girl with ADHD (attention deficit hyperactivity disorder), I couldn't conform correctly, either.

Self-hatred became my natural inclination.

It crept in quietly enough. The women in my life nitpicked my appearance until I learned what parts of me to hide. They frowned at baggy, worn clothes but yelled if they saw too much skin or traces of my figure. The men in my life silenced me until I learned not to speak. They ridiculed me for being "quiet and weird" but laughed when I tried to jump into conversations and ignored me when I asked questions. The contradictions exhausted me. I carved *I am always too much, but never enough* into every fiber of my being. I became equally scared of trying and not trying, so, whenever I could, I froze.

I grew into self-hatred. When I saw myself as a child, my first reaction was distaste. When I took on responsibilities, my heart pounded with panic. When I thought of my successes, unease washed over me that whatever fluke led to them would eventually be exposed. When I thought of my failures, my first reaction was smug, cognitively dissonant satisfaction: *I was right to doubt myself.* I felt irresponsible, unoriginal, unwanted, and destined for mediocrity; I didn't believe I was significant enough for anything better or worse.

If you've had similar thoughts, perhaps self-love does not come naturally to you, either. Whether by nature, nurture, or a combination of both, our immediate reactions to ourselves—the first, conditioned thoughts we have about our identity, physicality, abilities, and value—are often cruel. My first thoughts ruled tyrannically for years. They sent me spiraling into tailspins of self-sabotage. That spiral looked like this:

Step 1: Develop a new opportunity (a relationship, responsibility, etc.).

Step 2: Realize I partially control the outcome of the new opportunity.

Step 3: Panic because my first thoughts tell me I cannot and will not do what I should do[10] with the portion of the new opportunity I control.

Step 4: Panic some more because my first thoughts tell me trusting someone/something else to handle the portion of the new opportunity that's out of my control is not safe.[11]

Step 5: Reject, abandon, avoid, and/or destroy the new opportunity.

Step 6: Fulfill whatever prophecy my first thoughts of self-hatred foretold: that I can't do anything right, that I'm lazy and irresponsible, etc.

The above cycle impacted me every day. No thought process escaped the cycle's wrath. For example, did I want to make breakfast? *Nope. Not allowed. I could burn the house down.* Did my employer want to promote me? *No chance. I should quit before*

---

10 Whatever *that* means.
11 Because rejection, change, failure, and the unknown are life-threatening evils according to my traumatized, ADHD brain.

I destroy my employer's entire organization with my incompetence. No matter what happened, good or bad, my first thoughts could turn every situation into a problem, a reflection of my inadequacies, or a justification for some element of my self-loathing. The version of self-love I knew as a teenager and young adult never helped. It seemed insincere. How was I supposed to create positive feelings about someone I feared, didn't trust, and didn't respect: *Myself?* All the affirmations and journaling exercises felt hollow. Looking in the mirror and affirming beauty you don't see and value you don't recognize feels like a farce. My inability to create what I thought was self-love (positive feelings about myself) despite my efforts and dedication deepened my lack of self-trust and self-confidence.

My first thoughts overpowered me. Everything I did to fix them fed them. I've been in therapy since I was a kid. *Who needs to be in therapy for over ten years?* I filled journals with affirmations and blew paychecks on face masks, but my self-hatred persisted. *Who fails at self-love?* My anger and fear grew. I didn't want to be this way, and I worked hard to try to change. I went to school, got a job, and did everything else I thought would lead to success and happiness. All those efforts created more stability in my life, which initially relieved me but ultimately frustrated me because my first thoughts remained vicious. It made no sense. I thought I did what I was "supposed" to do. Why was my mind still so unkind?

That's the thing about self-hatred: you can't just wish it away, no matter how hard you try. So many factors contribute to self-hatred: systemic, cultural, psychological. **Deeply ingrained, reinforced self-hatred doesn't disappear overnight.** You probably won't like yourself right away after years of hating, neglecting, denying, or hiding from yourself, and that's okay. **Let go of that expectation.**

Learning how to love and care for yourself is a process. First, you have to define what love means to you not only as a feeling but also as a framework to guide action. What actions do you take or resist taking when you love yourself? Why and how do those actions improve your quality of life? How do you assess and meet your basic needs every day? If you've never thought about these things before, you may not know the answers immediately. Plus, your answers will probably change as you grow. Different seasons of your life require different kinds of love and care. All your needs won't stay exactly the same for your whole life because *you* won't stay exactly the same for your whole life.

Take your time. I spent years learning how to love and care for myself and how to differentiate positive feelings about myself from true self-love. I learn more and adjust as who I am and what I need changes. The truth behind such changes—the concept that evolution and adaptation are the only true constants—once terrified me, but I am learning to trust and celebrate it. Sometimes I embrace change with open arms. Sometimes I resist it, regress or stagnate, and that's okay. Progress doesn't have to be fast or linear. Progress doesn't require perfection. Allow yourself to grow at your own pace.

You and I were not born hating ourselves. We learned to hate, fear, dislike, or distrust ourselves, but we can learn to love, value, respect, trust, and accept ourselves, too. You and I are not the first people to struggle with self-love, especially the superficial, commodified version of self-love promoted online and in the media. Self-love is not just a positive feeling. Self-love is not the complete absence of negative emotions and insecurities. Self-love is not permanent, infallible happiness. It's something else entirely, and it's something that can be learned, applied, and changed. It's something you can tweak until it feels right.

You did not *fail*, and you are not *failing* at self-love.

You are not *bad* at self-love.
You are not *hard* to love.
You are *human*.

We're all human! Our moods morph. Circumstances change. Self-esteem fluctuates, even for the most confident, secure people. No matter how much we love ourselves, our first thoughts (our conditioned responses) can be negative, cruel, or unsettling sometimes. That doesn't mean we love ourselves any less. Love isn't just joy and pleasure. It's dedication. It's compassion. It's showing up for yourself even when things get hard and giving yourself grace when you have nothing else to give. Self-love means something different for everyone. I hope this book helps you begin to consider and understand what self-love means for you.

OUR SECOND THOUGHTS

Social media sells self-love like snake oil, like a magic elixir capable of curing all. Years ago, I bought into it. I internalized the toxic positivity slogan that everything must have a silver lining. I thought the only reason I couldn't love myself was because I hadn't tried hard enough yet. I never stopped to consider the irony in that. I never stopped to ask what love and happiness meant *to me*. I never researched other intrapersonal concepts like self-esteem. I didn't think it was necessary at the time. I thought self-love, self-esteem, and self-worth were all the same. I thought self-love was all or nothing. I thought you either loved yourself or you didn't, and I thought people who did lived in total happiness 24-7, 365 days a year. I wanted that perpetual love and joy for myself. I was desperate enough to try anything to achieve it. Alas, none of the aesthetically pleasing self-love tips recommended by social media erased my trauma or reversed years of operant conditioning. That's the problem. I put a Band-Aid on a bullet wound and blamed my application of the Band-Aid, not the Band-Aid's inadequacy, when the wound festered.[12]

I first encountered the phrase *self-acceptance* on TikTok, a video-sharing app, in 2020. My For You Page (TikTok's main video feed) refreshed. The video disappeared, but that phrase buried itself in the back of my mind.

Self-acceptance. *Not* self-love.

Days dragged into weeks during the COVID-19 quarantine. Self-acceptance chipped away at my curiosity. I slowly opened my mind to it. It was not self-love, the thing I thought I'd failed at. No, self-acceptance was something different. Something new. Something that could maybe, just maybe help me be a little bit kinder to myself. That's all I really wanted: a way to coexist with my first thoughts and create a more peaceful life. In 2020, I hesitantly hoped self-acceptance could help me. Four years later, self-acceptance is both a major reason why and how I wrote this book.

Self-acceptance does not have to come naturally to you. It's a skill we can practice and build, like training a muscle or learning a language. It doesn't require us to feel guilty about unlearning conditioned responses, which is hard and can take years. My first thoughts are indifferent at best and cruel at worst, but my first thoughts are not my responsibility. They exist. I disagree with them. That's all there is to it. I am responsible for my *next* thoughts, the thoughts that arise in response to my first thoughts, the thoughts that gently question, challenge, and negate my conditioning without making me feel ashamed or afraid of it. I call

---

12 To be clear, this is a metaphor for how singular acts of superficial self-care cannot fix self-hatred. I did not literally put a physical bandage on a physical wound.

these my second thoughts. If we practice observing, interrupting, challenging, redirecting, and disagreeing with our first thoughts before they reinforce harmful mind-sets and behaviors, we can slowly learn how to accept our first thoughts without judgment and exercise our autonomy in our second thoughts.

We may never unwaveringly adore ourselves and our bodies, but we don't have to. We're human. Our thoughts and feelings oscillate. We deserve love and care in the form of met needs regardless of feelings of worthiness or unworthiness. We can flex curiosity like a new muscle even if we aren't ready to put weight on it yet by considering alternatives to our conditioned responses even if we aren't sure how to act on or believe them yet. We can study multiple intrapersonal concepts and analyze how they work together to create more accessible and sustainable self-care systems. We can examine the interactions between self-love, self-care, self-focus, self-regulation, self-concept, self-acceptance, self-esteem, and self-worth to better understand how to build compassionate relationships with ourselves to improve our quality of life.

You don't have to change *who* you are to love yourself.

You can change *how* you love yourself, how you *understand* and *engage in* self-love.

HOW TO READ THIS BOOK

This book contains two parts. Part I features poetry. Part II features prose. I wrote the poems in Part I to capture a magical, fun feeling while still advocating for my beliefs. I wrote Part II to be the resource my younger self needed.[13]

---

13 And a resource for my current and future selves, too, evidently. I reread Part II several times while editing only to realize I wasn't living by my own standards. I mean it when I say I'm still learning. I'm right here with you in the trenches, my dear.

A younger me went to therapy. She was aware of self-love in theory. She was partially aware of her trauma and how it impacted her. But she had no idea how to love or care for herself on a daily basis. She possessed a plethora of information and misinformation, a cornucopia of contradictions, and it overwhelmed her. She needed something simple. She needed a one-stop shop to explain what works, what doesn't, and how it all connects so she could actually apply the information. Part II is that one-stop shop.

Part II offers four nonfiction chapters about my journey to accept myself; the interactions between self-love, self-care, and self-esteem; structural barriers to self-worth; and a concluding overview of how everything connects and can be applied (that's the Growth Guide). It contains writing prompts to help you reflect on the ideas presented and start the process of determining which ideas (if any) you want to apply to your own life. Part II also addresses some serious subjects, like mental health, neglect, and feelings of self-loathing, but it does not contain any explicit references, depictions, or detailed retellings of any occurrences that may be triggering to some audiences.

Part I offers rhyming poetry designed to help you see different parts of yourself and your body from new perspectives. Gratitude, love, and celebration uplift us. I include these themes in some poems, but this is not necessarily what everyone wants or needs. Not everyone feels grateful for their body. Sometimes our bodies can't or won't do what we want them to do. Not everyone loves or feels grateful for their life. Sometimes existence drains or pains us. If you struggle to find reasons to feel good about yourself and/or your life, I did, too.[14] Attempting to force positive spins on

---

14 I still do sometimes, but it doesn't scare me as much anymore. I know emotional states come and go, no matter the intensity of the emotion or apathy in the moment.

my pain frustrated me and inevitably made me feel worse. I don't want to make anyone feel that way, so I aim to balance the positive with the negative when I write (which I believe reflects the reality of the human experience).

If all you've ever known is hatred, conceptualizing love seems impossible. Forget about feeling it. You're trying to enter a state of being that opposes your past and current states of being. You're trying to do something unfamiliar, something that your subconscious might fear or resist even if you consciously want it. Consider incremental change, too. Shifting from hatred to dislike or from dislike to neutrality might be more achievable first steps. Considering the absence of hatred as a possibility even if you can't conceptualize love is also a good place to start. I wrote these poems to propose alternatives to self-hatred and neutral perspectives about ourselves and our bodies in addition to positive perspectives. Folks who follow me online requested the topics of several poems in Part I. These are the fairy godmother poems, the poems that changed my life in the most magical ways.

Have fun when you read these poems. I wrote them to be read aloud. If you read this book aloud yourself, I highly recommend reading the poems with a fun accent or voice. Personally, I prefer a posh British or transatlantic accent (think Katharine Hepburn and Bette Davis). Do whatever's the most fun for you.

Now, without further ado, let's toast to you with a poem I wrote JUST **for you** and certainly not at all to help us transition tonally from this introduction to Part I:

TO THE WONDERFULLY
WORTHY PERSON
READING THIS:

Be who you are
(whoever that may be),
and may you have the strength
to be you proudly.

Only you can be you
(it's cheesy but true).
Only you make life magical
the way that you do.

PART 1
Poetry

The Universe's Muse

If your skin has scars, stretch marks, or tints of blue,
purple, green, brown, red, or gray that stir insecurity in you,
look around, my dear. See yourself in Earth's every hue.

Your blues and reds are the scarlet sun shining over the
    sapphire seas.
Your purples and greens are the violet veins lining the leaves
    on the trees.
Your grays and browns are the foggy foam settling over the
    sepia sand.
You are the beauty buried in the sea, soaring in the sky, and
    living in the land.

You are all the Earth. The sun and stars. The Universe's muse.
She molds you with her light and paints the planets with your
    hues.

We Do Not Detract from Each Other

You watch the rain carve rivers on your window
with the same adoring eyes you use to see
the sunset's painted purple, pink clouds,
and you love both beauties equally.

You, the rivers and rain,
and they, the horizon and sun:
the Earth needs you both to bloom.
Together, your gifts help us grow as one.

Thank You for Eating with Me

To stay alive, you have to eat.
Here's some fun food facts
that make eating pretty neat:

Powerful protein helps us move
and makes our muscles strong.
Cool carbohydrates and friendly fats
energize us to dance to our favorite songs.
Food fuels us, carries culture and tradition,
and keeps us warm in rainy weather.
If eating gets hard, I'm here for you.
If you want, we can take a bite together.

On the count of three, I'll take my bite.
Once you're ready, you can take yours, too.
I know you can't see me, my food, or my fork,
but you can trust me to do what I say I'll do.
I trust you to take your bite today
whenever you're ready, even if I can't see it.
I've got my food now. Once you have yours,
we'll eat together. Let's count of three it:

1!
2!
3!

Thank you for eating with me.

Teatime

You will never be *everyone's* cup of tea,
so you may as well be *your own* cup of tea.

Why ruin how the tea tastes to *you*
for people who don't even drink it?

Identi-tea

Love who you love. Be who you are.
Whether you feel that you're near or far
from embracing your identity,
you have time to become
who you're meant to be.

You, one day, will wake up and say,
"I am found, at peace. I am me this way."

Unconditional Love

My love is not something you must earn.
You already have it. You always have
and always will.
I have loved you since before time began,
and when time ends,
I will love you still.

Adjectives vs. Insults

To me, "fat" is not an insult.
Neither is "skinny" nor "midsize."
They're simply words that we can use
to describe our bodies and size.

These words don't have to be cruel
just because someone says they are.
The idea that one person could force everyone
to think the same thing is a bit bizarre.

You decide what these words mean to you.
Others decide what these words mean to them, too,
whether they're neutral, mean, or kind.
Set your own boundaries,
respect others' wishes,
and keep good manners in mind.

Scars & Stars

If your body is home to some scars,
no matter what they're from,
you are still made of the dust of stars,
and the cosmos love what their creation has become.

Your scars don't make you any less *you*,
and bodies of all kinds deserve to be seen.
Our scars, our differences, our lumps and bumps:
these things make us human. They are not obscene.

An Anxious Guarantee

If you have social anxiety or generalized anxiety like me,
I won't insult you and say it'll magically get better,
but I can and will make you a guarantee.

No matter how our anxious brains catastrophize,
no matter what we say, what we do or do not do,
at the end of the day, people worry much more about
themselves and their own lives than they worry about me or you.

If you tried your best, and your intentions were pure,
then you did what any good human would do.
When we mess up, we make amends
and try again. We learn and grow.
That's all anyone can ask of you.

ODES TO APHRODITE

Rockin' & Rollin'

If you have fat rolls, let me tell you something true.
Aphrodite rocked fat rolls on her back and stomach, too.
Legend says that Aphrodite changed her form so she could appear
beautiful by anyone's standards, which you may have deduced, my dear,
means the Greek goddess of beauty herself knows how ethereal rolls can be
and that beauty is subjective and shines in all of us in various ways uniquely.

Heavenly Hip-Dips

If you have hip-dips, I have
something to share with you.
Did you know Aphrodite's
heavenly hips depict dips, too?

If the goddess of romance, beauty, and love
proudly has hip-dips, well then, my little dove,
you can, too, and I encourage you to do
whatever the radiant Aphrodite would do*.

*WITHIN REASON! No war starting.

Remember Your Worth

Whether you're fat, thin, or midsize,
with big or small thighs,
I need you to realize that you are a prize*,
and you deserve to be treated as such.

*But not a prize to be won, as a certain magic carpet–riding princess asked me to make clear.

Perfectly Proportioned Partners

You can be bigger than your partner
no matter your gender or theirs.
Is the relationship healthy? Are you happy?
If you are, forget size! Genuinely, my dear, who cares?

I say this now, but I once worried about size, too.
My bigness used to fill me with romantic strife.
I've been five ten (taller than most American men)
and a hefty weight my whole adult life . . .

. . . but that's never stopped the short kings from courting me,
nor has it ever fazed someone who truly loved me.
The right person for us will love who we are first
and secondarily find our features lovely.

Think of everything your partner dislikes about themselves.
Now think of how you see them in a different light.
Your partner sees you the way you lovingly see them,
and that includes your size, shape, weight, and height.

For All the Brothers

(But Mostly Mine)

Dear big and little brothers:
You don't always have to be strong.
Men can be many things, *anything!*
Be your true self, and you won't go wrong.

You're a magnificent man
whether you rock facial hair or a clean shave,
and all the toughest men know it's okay to cry.
To feel is to be alive. To express, you must be *brave.*

You can be soft whenever you want or need.
You can be sad, be held. You can ask for help.
If you want, you can keep your feelings and thoughts private,
or you can speak freely about your mental health.

You can lift weights, run, or play sports.
You can practice performance, dance, or sing.
You can study history, art, planes, or makeup.
You can spend your time exploring or creating anything.

There is no right or wrong way to be a man.
Your fears and dreams matter just as much as everyone's.
You are enough. You are already the kind of man
anyone would be proud to call
brother,
father,
son.

"I Am Fat"

When I say, "I am fat,"
it's not an insult or compliment.
It's simply a statement of fact.
I have some flab,
but I don't look drab.
In fact, I think I look fab!
I'm fat, nonetheless, and
please don't make this a contest
of "Who's fatter or thinner?"
We ALL deserve dinner.
We ALL look like winners.
Some of us just happen to be fat.

Stomach Sizes

Our stomachs can be small.
Our stomachs can be wide.
Our midsections can be thin, fat, flat,
or round on either side.

Fairy godmothers aren't allowed to lie.
I swear on my wand that my words reign true.
I think your midsection, be it toned or tubby,
looks lovely because it is a part of you.

Besties & Boundaries

If you call yourself fat, I won't argue with that
because "fat" is not a bad word to me.
To me, "fat" is a neutral descriptor
unrelated to worth, beauty, or morality.

The word fat has been used to harm and harass some folks,
so some people prefer to describe themselves in other ways.
Some people don't want their body or identity mentioned at all,
regardless of the intention behind a conversation, question,
or phrase.

It's important to respect people's preferences.
Avoiding hurtful topics is not a difficult task.
If you're ever unsure about a friend's boundaries,
when in doubt, you can politely ask.

I see my best friends for lunch every Thursday.
We know each other well, but when we sit down, we still say:
"I'm so happy to see you! I've got so much to tell you!
Real quick, are there any topics we should avoid today?"

Some people say this is unnecessary or awkward,
but for me and my best friends, it gets the job done.
It helps us respect and understand each other, which we *want* to do.
We love each other! We want everyone
to feel safe, to feel seen, and to have fun.

Be Your Own Bestie First

Not everyone will like you.
If that scares you,
let me tell you something true:

You do not have to be liked by *everyone*
as long as you are liked by you.
(But, for the record, I think
you're very cool as well.)

For the Chronically Ill

If you're chronically ill,
you're not a pill.
You're not a burden or bad.

You're a wonderful, worthy human being,
no matter what health struggles you've had.

Functionality and ability do not make us who we are.
It's our inner light that shines forth from within
that truly makes us stars.

Foreheads and Fiveheads

If you have a forehead,
a fivehead,
a wide head,
or perhaps you've a forehead that's
asymmetrically divided,
no matter how it looks,
it houses your thoughts and brain,
and it's home to the magical impulses
that tell you to dance in the rain.

Personally, I've got a fine fivehead.
I've been called *Megamind* once or twice.
It hurt when I was younger, but I laugh at it now.
My fivehead and I grew up to be funny, smart, and
nice.

A Heartbreak Healing Recipe

If your heart is broken,
you may wonder how to heal it.
When my heart hurts, it doesn't heal
until I allow myself to feel it.

First, identify the specifics of your pain.
What caused it? How does your emotional pain *physically* feel?
Next, let yourself cry, shout, write, run, rest—do whatever you
can to safely release the pain you previously concealed.

Now, be as patient as possible with yourself.
Healing is not linear. It won't happen overnight.
Some days you'll feel cured, some days you'll still hurt,
and some days you'll just be all right.

This is all part of being human.
Tend to your heart. Love will wait for you.
Give it time to appear.
You have nothing to fear.
There is so much magic still
manifesting for you, my dear.

Your Romantic Nose

If you aren't a fan of your nose
because of its shape or size,
you must remember why your nose is your nose,
why most noses are not molded for modern eyes.

Your nose curves with culture and ancestral meaning.
Your nose helped many people find and fall in love.
Your nose holds every hello that led to you.
Love lives and breathes in your bones,
my dear little dove.

Your Thighs Are the Prize

If you don't like your thighs,
there must be something in your eyes,
because I think your thighs are wonderful
no matter your thighs' size.
You can rock thunder thighs,
thin thighs, or thighs full of muscle.
You can rock thick thighs,
thighs with cellulite, or thighs without muscle.
Whether you walk or get around in a chair,
your thighs are worthy, this I swear.

Almighty Arms

Whether your arms are big and round like mine
or your arms are short and thin, my dear,
you're still divine.
Whether it's loose skin, muscle, or fat,
if your arms are tight or you have
wings like a bat,
you are incredible through and through.
Your almighty arms are incredible, too.

May I Suggest a Selection of Swimsuits?

If you're worried about wearing a swimsuit,
I have some ideas that we can talk through.

I personally think you're perfect,
but I know swimsuit season can be scary.
That's why I keep my selection of swimsuits well stocked
to help me feel water-ready, not water-wary.

There's the American classics:
one-pieces, swim trunks, and bikinis.
There's also swim shirts, skirts,
hooded swim wraps, and tankinis.
There's full-body wet suits
and suits with sleeves
for folks who burn easy.
There's suits designed to keep you
covered and modest,
and there's suits designed to be
free and breezy.

If you don't find any swimsuits you feel comfortable wearing,
remember, you can always use a cover-up or rock regular
clothes.
In my opinion, you should wear whatever you need or want to
so you can splash around safely and feel the sand between your
toes.

Divine Jawline

Your double chin is not a sin,
and your soft jawline is divine.
As features go, it's not ugly or bad,
and, at some point, it's one everyone's had or will have.
Whether your jawline is genetic, arrived with age,
or came with changes in weight,
it has no impact on your worth,
and that is never up for debate.

Tooth Gaps

If you've got a tooth gap,
I do, too!
There's all kinds of other people
who also belong to the tooth-gap crew.

Models with tooth gaps walk the runway
and represent beauty that's raw and real.
They know that their tooth gaps add
to their unique, eye-catching appeal.

Your body is your own. That includes your teeth.
What you do with your gap is up to you.
Your smile is beautiful because it's *kind*,
and, gap or no gap, that will always be true.

Smile Insecurity

If you dislike your smile,
let me tell you a tale
about a girl with a tooth gap and stained teeth
whose confidence used to be frail.

I hated my smile for many years.
People seeing my teeth was a deep fear
until I got older and one day realized
my smile may not be perfect to everyone's eyes,
but seeing it can still cheer their hearts and lift their moods.
Now, I smile and laugh freely, and I don't worry
about anyone being rude.

Hair Texture

If you don't like your hair,
may I ask you why?

Forgive me for being bold,
but according to my eyes
your hair is lovely
no matter how much or how little you have,
no matter the color, shape, or silhouette size
or what texture the strands have
because your hair belongs to you,
and I think we both know it's true
that everything you are is lovely.
Lovely is everything that you do.

Body Hair

Hair can grow anywhere on your body,
on your limbs, head, back, chest, stomach, face, and birth-
    marks,
but you don't have to hide, cut, wax, remove, or keep it,
whether it's thin, straight and light, or thick, curly, and
    dark.

One day you may want all your hair gone.
A different day, you may want to grow it out.
Both choices are okay. Your body is your business.
You deserve respect with hair or without.

Acne & Pimples

Acne and pimples do not mean we're unclean,
and they certainly don't mean we shouldn't be seen!
Our skin is not made to be flawless paper or porcelain.
It's an organ meant to grow and morph and be lived in.
Whether your breakouts are constant, hormonal,
                            or occasional,
        they are still part of you, and you, my dear,
                            are sensational.

You Are Never Too Old for Magic

Do you remember me, my dear?
I see the changes in your face from the years.
I feel the ache in your heart.

I came to remind you
life is not always like this,
and, though it may not seem so,
life will not always be
as gray as it may feel right now.
If you ever need a bit of magic,
close your eyes.
Search your heart.

Make a wish,
and remember me.

We Are Not Too Much

It's funny how people call us
too fat, too thin, *too much*
to make us feel like
we aren't enough.
It's strange how they hiss,
"Stand up for yourself"
but insist we lower our fists
when we call their bluff.

I've tried to be what they want me to be,
but I tire of being unseen.
I will no longer hide for the sake of their eyes.
My body, my existence, is not obscene.

Farewell, Part I

Is it surprising that we talk so loudly
yet say so little when there was
safety in our silence?

We resent the quiet that permitted their sins
but remember the consequences of cacophony.
Now, we bellow back into the blue,
full of the fury inherited in our initials.
We demand damages for our neglected needs,
but we don't know how to hold hope,
how to keep kindness from crumbling
in the clutches of our outstretched claws.

I don't know what you expect this to be,
but I'll do the terrifying. I'll be known.
I'll be true.

I will be me if you promise you'll try,
at least here with me,
to be you.

PART 2
Prose

CHAPTER 1

WHEN LIFE GIVES YOU LEMONS, FIND YOUR FAIRY GODMOTHER
(How I Slowly, Painfully Learned All This Stuff)

The sun blinds and burns the first time you step into its light after living in the dark. It is unfamiliar, frightening. It blisters. In the face of the unknown, shadows beckon you back. A decision looms. Will you return to what you know, to the cold, dark familiar, or will you brave this bright new world? You hesitate, frozen in fear. How can you survive a world that opposes all you've ever known? Analysis paralysis loosens its grip on you as the searing sunbeams soothe into warm, radiant rays and thaw your frozen limbs. Your eyes adjust to the light. Shapes solidify on the horizon. The chaotic, overwhelming unknown calms into a curious concept. What once burned and blinded now warms and welcomes you. You do not race forward, but you do not rush back. You stand still in your consideration, and that is enough.

Do not let familiarity fool you. You don't have to plunge head-first into the unknown. A hesitant step, a whispered *what-if*, a single shining second of hope amid a sea of despair is all fate needs to plant the seeds of change within us. Even still, I resisted change until fate forced my hand.

Life ground to a screeching halt in the spring of 2020. The first COVID-19 shutdown knocked all the professional, academic, and personal commitments I juggled right out of my hands. University campuses closed. Offices went virtual. Time froze. None of us knew what would happen at the end of those initial two weeks.

Would the world go back to the way it was?

Could it?

Should it?

We watched. We waited. We worried.

We hung suspended as others searched for answers.

For the first time in years, I cautiously considered rest. I wasn't overbooked. I had nowhere to go. Nothing to do. The pandemic prevented me from overextending myself like I had for most of my life. Still, I resisted rest and waited for a verdict. Would life go back to the way it was? I needed to be ready if it did. I felt like I hadn't earned the right to rest yet, like it wasn't safe to stop, so I initially fought to keep my draining, destructive pre-COVID-19 routines alive while socially distancing. I didn't know what else to do. Familiarity felt safer than the unknown, and I was most familiar with stress. I'd never stopped moving before. I feared who I might become if I lost years of momentum.

My university closed and switched to virtual learning for the rest of that semester. They introduced a pass-fail grading system to accommodate for unexpected travel and technical difficulties. On-campus jobs shut down, as did most extracurriculars. All the standards and systems that dictated my pre-pandemic life dissolved.

I grew up with omnipresent anxiety, PTSD (post-traumatic stress disorder), and undiagnosed attention-deficit/hyperactivity disorder. I relied on chronic stress, adrenaline, and cortisol to do everything. Fear pushed me to work, to unfreeze. I put myself in high-pressure positions and situations because it was the only way to ensure I did anything at all. I carried that habit with me from high school all the way to my first post collegiate job. I wasn't consciously aware of this phenomenon at the time, which served me well in some ways. External pressure helped me achieve things my self-loathing urged me to sabotage. But you can't live sustainably this way, caught in a perpetual ping-pong match between stress and self-loathing and depression and avoidance. Eventually, the ball drops.

Everything came crashing down when COVID-19 hit. I once obsessed over maintaining a perfect GPA, but that semester I barely mustered the energy to attend a single virtual class. I opted in to my university's pass-fail system. My numeric grades plummeted. I did what work I could to guarantee I'd pass. Then, I waved my white flag and collapsed into burnout. I lay down with no intention of ever getting back up.

Life Gave Me . . . Lemons?
Days bled into weeks as I slept. The more I rested, the worse I felt. There was nothing left to distract me from my battered body and brain. I couldn't ignore reality anymore. I felt *awful*. My stomach churned. My head pounded. My body ached. My skin and scalp itched. My hair broke easily, often. I hardly recognized myself in the mirror.

Sometimes curiosity gnawed at my reflection's attention. Lockdown had lasted only about a month at this point. I refused to think about much then, but I almost let myself wonder: How long had I *really* been like this? How long had I been so unwell without realizing it? I stared at myself and teetered on the brink of action before extinguishing my curiosity. I forbade myself from caring. I swung from one extreme to the other.

I used to do and care about everything.

Then I did and cared about nothing.

I holed up in my room. I had no desire or reason to venture out into the world. Basic toiletries and groceries weren't worth the trip. Social distancing and the isolation of a codependent relationship metastasized into apathy and paranoia. My former self shriveled. I stopped speaking to family and friends. I didn't trust anyone, including myself. I tried to will the paranoia and discomfort away. It festered. Once it grew too sharp to sleep through, my pain annoyed me into action. It disrupted my hibernation, and that was the last straw. I huffed and puffed. I complained about it, but I rolled up my sleeves and got to work.

I wasn't sure why my body hurt. I didn't have a doctor. Or a dentist, therapist, or psychiatrist, for that matter. I hadn't seen anyone for anything in years. I just knew I felt awful, and I wanted it to stop. I wanted to go back to sleep. Since I couldn't consult a professional, I researched my symptoms online.

Suggestions about the severity of my condition alarmed me. Catastrophizing thoughts cooed between my ears. Certain websites try to convince you that you've got stage-four cancer instead of the common cold. One second you have a mild runny nose, and the next you're spiraling down a hypochondriac rabbit hole because a website with a bunch of affiliate marketing links told you to say your final farewells before it's too late. I knew to expect and avoid this. Even still, the true toll of neglecting my needs boiled in the pit of my stomach. At best, my symptoms meant something bad was brewing. At worst, it was already upon me.

My apathy kept me somewhat objective. I made a list of the notable family medical histories.[15] It consisted of heart disease,

---

15 I make lots of lists. Lists, charts, graphs, webs. I like to organize most things *except* the back seat of my car. Whatever gets abandoned back there is, frankly, none of my business.

diabetes, mental illnesses, and cancer. Lots and lots of cancer, often fatal cancer. I stared at my list. It stared back at me. Maybe it was the paranoia. Maybe it was the isolation. Maybe it was my overactive imagination, but I swear the list whispered:

"Well . . . what now?"

What now, indeed, little list?

In terms of clues, I lacked even the foggiest.

The links between chronic stress, trauma, neglected needs, and my mysterious physical pains evaded me. Stress at school and work served as welcome distractions from stress at home. I failed to see and understand the connection between the fear that defined my private life and the pressure and panic that sustained my public life. These two concepts—unaddressed, ongoing trauma and seeking out high-pressure situations—existed in different categories in my conscious mind, but both environments triggered constant states of fight-or-flight.

For the first twenty-one years of my life, I cared for myself minimally, reluctantly, and resentfully. Early childhood experiences established an insidious belief in me that I did not deserve to feel safe. Other unescapable, continuous circumstances reinforced that belief and instilled a sense of perpetual uncleanliness within me that made hygiene feel pointless and infuriating. I did what I could to keep myself presentable enough to avoid arousing too much outside suspicion.

Rest filled me with guilt. Only physical illnesses kept me from going to class or work. Even then, I only rested long enough to restore a minimal amount of energy. Once I got that adrenaline-and-cortisol cocktail back up and running, I was "cured," as far as I was concerned. Panic made me productive, so the rest of the world seemed to consider me cured, too. As I got older, I internalized that academic and career success mattered more than almost anything else. I thought it was fine, even admirable, to neglect my needs in the name of productivity. I didn't see this as sacrificing my health. If anything, my needs annoyed me. I mean, come *on*! Do humans *really* have to eat, sleep, and maintain hygiene every day?

Evidently, yes.

I hadn't yet realized the underlying cause of my physical symptoms, but I had a pretty hefty hunch that it might be lack of self-care. Not the commodified, sparkly kind of self-care that dominates social media. I mean actual self-care, as in literally taking care of my being and body by consistently meeting my basic needs. By the time COVID-19 hit, school, work, and extracurriculars had consumed me so deeply that I couldn't remember the last time I ate without urgency or walked anywhere other than to and from class, my dorm, or my car.

I cut myself a deal: I'd heal over the summer. I couldn't return to my normal jobs yet anyway because of the pandemic, so I had the time and just enough money saved up to pull it off.[16] It would be the first job-free summer since I started babysitting as a preteen. I committed myself to my health. But only so I could resume hibernating, of course. I would never *dream* of taking care of myself just for the sake of improving my quality of life. How selfish. The *scandal* of the mere *suggestion*, my dear![17]

I reassessed my pain. My muscles, stomach, and head hurt the most. They took priority. Futile attempts to soothe my pain with quick fixes ended in frustration. I felt like I was learning infant care again. Here was this living, breathing human staring at me,

---

16 Which was a huge privilege, one I did not take lightly. It quite literally wouldn't have been possible for me to explore self-care without my newfound free time. Free time is a resource, just like money, that not everyone has in equal amounts.

17 That's a joke, to be clear. I know tone can be tough to detect, especially in text. It is for me, at least. Whoever designed my character nerfed my social stats before they booted me up on Earth.

trusting me to fulfill her needs, and all I could do was blink back at her. Humans are so much harder than academics. Everything you know seems so far away when someone peers into your soul with a gaze that says, "I trust you with my *life*. Please handle it with care," especially when the person gazing at you *is you*. You are both the responsibility bearer and consequence receiver of potential mistakes.

I decided to start with the basics to minimize risk. If I drank more water, ate regularly, and moved my muscles a bit, maybe I'd be able to sleep again. I enacted my plan the next morning by going on a short walk.

The hot Florida sun blistered against the back of my neck. Sweltering sunbeams sizzled down from the sky and blinded me every time the clouds shifted. I wanted to run right back to my cold, familiar bedroom. I grumbled and forced myself to keep walking. *Do it for the sake of our aching muscles*, I told myself. *Do it so we can go back to bed.*

I wasn't happy about it.

I wasn't grateful for it.

I was anxious and annoyed, but I did it anyway. I knew it would help in the long run, no matter how much it sucked in the moment.

Walking shocked me. For years, I'd told myself I didn't have the time or energy for things like a daily walk. I thought unnecessary daily exertions would drain me. Walking surprised me by doing the opposite. It energized me. I stayed outside a bit longer every time I left my room. I smiled when the sun greeted me. She sparkled and sang the first time I planted my bare feet in the grass by the sidewalk. My inner critic wailed about how ridiculous I looked and begged me to put my shoes back on. I told her to pipe down. I didn't want her nagging to interrupt the whoosh of the wind whistling through the palm trees.

I stumbled upon an Einstein Bros. Bagels during one of my walks. I got a breakfast bagel on a whim. Two birds with one stone: movement and a meal. That bacon, egg, and cheese bagel was so good that I went back and got the same thing the next day. I wolfed the bagel down while I walked and chugged some water to cool off once I got home.

I showered after every walk. The sweat irritated me otherwise. They weren't long or fancy showers. Soap up. Rinse off. Get out. I didn't have separate face and body washes. I didn't apply any skin-care products post shower, either. I didn't care. I was showering, moving, hydrating, and eating. *Consistently.* I cried quietly into my bagel the morning I realized I'd walked, showered, and eaten breakfast five days in a row.

Using external stress and pressure as my primary motivators made me feel like a bitter failure for two reasons. First, I prioritized what others asked me to do instead of doing what I genuinely wanted to do, which wasn't fair to anyone (including myself) and led me to quietly resent people who didn't do anything other than ask for my time.[18] Second, I felt like I never fully delivered on my promises. I did nearly everything at the last minute regardless of the scale of the promise, which meant something had to give (usually a degree of quality). Even when I exceeded everyone else's expectations, I never measured up to my own because I knew I could've done more.[19]

But look!

Here was self-care, something I wanted and decided to do for myself—not because anybody else told me to—and I followed through. Not just once. Not just at the last minute. I moved, nourished, and cleansed my body first thing in the morning every

18 I didn't know how to say no to people without feeling guilty yet.
19 *Believed* is the correct word, but at the time I treated my perceived shortcomings like facts, not subjective beliefs.

day. EVERY DAY. I created *and* maintained a self-care routine. I promised myself I'd do this. I trusted myself to do it. And I did it. I actually did it!

The pride, relief, and curiosity that washed over me fueled me to dive deeper into self-care. If a self-care routine as simple as a morning walk, breakfast, and shower uplifted me this much, imagine what better sleep, nutrition, and skin care could do. Forget the original plan. I didn't want to withdraw, hide, or hibernate anymore.

I wanted to get better.

I taught myself very basic skin care. I applied sunscreen before my walk, lotion after my shower, and night cream before bed. I kept it simple enough to ensure it only took a total of ten extra minutes a day at *maximum*. My raw, inflamed skin stopped itching. The cracks smoothed. The redness cooled.

I forced myself to get over my fear of stovetops and learned how to cook meals that tasted good and nourished me. I realized I'm not as picky of an eater as my family alleged. I *like* vegetables. I just want them prepared a certain way. Do you know what it's like to taste oven-roasted veggies prepared with olive oil, garlic, salt, cracked pepper, chili powder, and paprika for the first time?

It's life-changing.

So is self-care. My pre-pandemic college commitments gave me fleeting hits of happiness and pride, but stress and exhaustion always loomed right around the corner. Self-care felt like a low-risk, high-reward infinity loop. The more I cared for myself, the better I felt. The better I felt, the more energy I had to care for myself. I even started to daydream again. I stopped cursing my imagination for distracting me and let it lead me as I walked, showered, and cooked. Memories of storytelling, singing, and playing pretend rushed back to me. I remembered who I wanted to be when I grew up. I wondered how I'd ever forgotten.

Writing exhilarated me for the first time in years. Worlds unfolded in my mind. Glee guided my giddy pen. Stories, poems, and music flowed out of me. I never stopped to question the quality of my creations. I created for the sake of creating. I felt like I could breathe again. Imagining and creating grew as central to my days as my morning walks. I couldn't fathom how I'd lived any other way for so long, so I cut myself a new deal: I'd heal *and* create over the summer. Then, when the world went back to the way it was before, I'd go back to the way I was before, too. I figured that I would've cared for my body enough by then that it could withstand the return to my previous lifestyle.

As the novelty of rediscovery subsided, anxiety about the "real" world stirred in the back of my mind. Creating and self-care were great, but what about my grades? What would I do after graduation? What *should* I do? How would I make money?

Unwilling to abandon my dreams or new way of life, I cut myself a third deal. If I could make my dreams financially viable, I'd pursue them after college. Plenty of artists supported themselves with their skills. Why couldn't I? I consolidated my passions for writing, singing, and performing into one all-encompassing dream: creating. I refused to entertain alternatives. I *knew* creating would sustain me. I would *make it* sustain me. Blindly, stubbornly, I believed in my plan's unproven potential, in *my* potential.

That's when I discovered TikTok.

Life Gave Me Rotten *Lemons?!*

Truthfully, I was already on TikTok, but I'd never posted myself. Fear and shame kept me from seriously considering it. After all, why would someone like me post themselves? Only celebrities and serious creators—people with skills or something to offer—posted regularly to social media. What would I even post? I couldn't dance. I wasn't virally pretty. Makeup confused and frustrated me. No one cared about what I had to say, and they certainly wouldn't want to see or hear me say it. Who did I think I was?

Insecurities and doubts like those above dominated my decisions pre-pandemic. My parents encouraged me to dream within reason. They knew the importance of passion but feared the world's cruelty. Dreams were risky. Mine had a high chance of failure. My parents tried to balance support with healthy realism, and so I learned to dream in theory but rarely in execution.

I inherited apprehension. Trauma left me terrified of the unknown and reinforced the narrative that authenticity led to pain. I feared using my voice and sharing my creations. I didn't want to be truly seen, to be known. It felt dangerous. So I hid. I stayed in school, maintained my GPA, worked, and planned for the future. The illusion of control promised a financially stable life in exchange for following the predictable path, and I drank the Kool-Aid. I buried the parts of myself I'd been conditioned to hate and fear under a more socially acceptable guise. Shrinking, silencing, and hiding myself became familiar, and the familiar felt safe.

My fears conflicted with the latest deal I'd cut myself. TikTok possessed the power to make and break people overnight, but posting myself contradicted every anxious and self-deprecating foundation of my identity. Photos and videos of myself forced me to face my physical appearance and left me lost in hypercritical, dysmorphic mazes of overthinking and self-loathing. I barely posted to social media. My life didn't feel interesting or important enough to capture, let alone to share. I occasionally posted academic or extracurricular achievements. Sometimes I shared family-and-friends group photos from special events. I posted the rare, painfully posed selfie to my story when I felt brave. In twenty-four hours, it disappeared, and I told myself no one would remember it anyway. Stories, successes, but *never* candid me. Never my personality. Why would I show the parts of me I wanted to hide?

The opportunity TikTok presented demanded that I confront these fears. I could have everything I wanted if I would just post myself. I could share my music, poems, and stories. I could write and act in my own skits. I could apply the knowledge gained from my multimedia journalism and digital marketing studies to monetize my skills and support my dreams. The reason for my blind faith materialized right in front of me. It was so close! There was just the teeny, tiny issue of my entire being, brain, and self-concept opposing the path forward. If I could get over that, I could have it all. Easy-peasy.

I'm an efficient, logical[20] person. I had already mastered self-care (so I thought). I'd healed my body (again, so I thought). In comparison to healing literal organs, how hard could working on my sense of self possibly be? I just needed a strategy. And a list, for good measure. I whipped out my notebook and devised my master plan:

Step 1: Identify the root of my self-hatred and its impact on my day-to-day life.

Step 2: Heal it.

Step 3: Achieve my dreams and live happily ever after.

As you may know if you've also tried to expedite your healing, it's shockingly not that simple. Several substeps hide between each of the main steps. Analyzing my day-to-day behaviors and

---

20 Impatient, pattern recognizing.

identifying harmful patterns led to more questions. For example, insecurity in my physical appearance often overwhelmed me. I hated seeing my face and body. I traced the root of this specific form of self-hatred back to generational and societal traumas. Growing up around adults who openly hated and criticized their own bodies, considered self-confidence arrogant, and "jokingly" criticized my body perfectly prepped me to believe the essential premise of diet culture: that my body is bad and needs to be changed. I mourned the loss of my innocence for about three seconds before I said, "All right, enough. Time for step two."

Since I hated my appearance, I decided to heal by improving my look. I'd transform into such a beautiful person that loving myself would be the only logical thing left to do.[21] The success of my current self-care practices made me confident I could take on even more. I had the morning routine down. Why wouldn't I add new hair, makeup, clothing, more complex skin care, oral hygiene, exercise, and meal routines all at once?

What could *possibly* go wrong?

My body and brain fought me each step of the way. Brushing my teeth annoyed me. Showering for longer than five minutes[22] exhausted me and felt like a waste of time and energy. Makeup? Oh, please. It wouldn't hide my asymmetrical eyebrows, the bump in my nose, or the elephant ears people told me to get pinned back. Why bother? Plus, no matter how well I took care of myself one day, I would still have to do it all again the next day. That concept anguished me.

What happened to my infinite loop of energy and good vibes? Why was it all going wrong? I was so elated about my original

---

21 Ah, poor younger me. All fired up and ready for change but missing the core concept.
22 The maximum duration of my "Soap up. Rinse off. Get out." showers.

progress that I forgot I was still new to self-care.[23] I forgot I'd only been recovering from a lifetime of neglect for ten days. I didn't give myself enough time to rest restoratively, not just while I was in pain, and I didn't give my self-care practices enough time to settle into stable, long-term routines before I demanded more of myself. I unknowingly actualized the ultimate irony: I overextended myself in the name of self-care. Burnout bubbled in the background. Desperation to fend off the brewing breakdown drove me to try harder, to use up the last of my already depleted energy, and launched me headfirst into defeat. Exhaustion eroded me into another detached, apathetic stupor accented by existential frustration. I felt like no matter how much I tried, it would never be enough.

I was stunned. Stumped. It didn't make sense. Why was I resisting what I thought was positive change? Why didn't I believe I was worthy of self-care? Why didn't I deserve to feel clean? I could take long showers, get dressed, and apply makeup to prepare for events, work, and school. I had no problem taking care of myself when *other people* would see me. Why couldn't I do it for *myself*? Why wasn't I worth the effort? Why wasn't I enough? I realized I'd have to answer all those questions before I could move on to step three of my master plan.

Ugh.

I tried. Each time I thought I found an answer, it turned out to be the mere tip of another unearthed iceberg. Each layer I peeled back revealed more grief and anger. Years of fear, operant conditioning, trauma, and unmet needs cooked at the core of it all. I remembered the question I dared not answer at the start of the pandemic:

How long had I *really* been like this?

I was frustrated. Furious. Heartbroken. TikTok's user base

---

23 And that I have ADHD and PTSD, which means my ability levels vary from day to day no matter how well I take care of myself.

grew by the day, but its organic reach[24] wouldn't be so generous forever. I felt the clock ticking. Determined not to miss my chance, I devised a compromise between my dreams and my fears. I posted low-risk content and hid the parts of myself I still hated. I followed audio trends. I used filters. I spoke in a higher, softer voice than normal in the rare videos where I used my voice. I gained about three hundred followers in a month, which was crazy compared to the humble follower count on my old, private social media accounts, but I lacked direction. I'd lost sight of the point. I wasn't sharing my music or poems or making skits. I was hiding again. What was it all for?

I found the body-positivity community on TikTok in April 2020. I'd encountered body-positive content before,[25] but I didn't know much about it beyond the occasional unposed poolside photo. Body-positive TikTok was different. As a video-first platform, TikTok allowed body-positive users to prioritize movement over static images. Creators shared videos of themselves eating, dancing, styling outfits, and taking up space. Sometimes they showed themselves proudly, confidently, and happily. Sometimes they showed themselves while scared, sad, or ashamed. No matter what, they showed themselves in videos, not just photos. They showed themselves moving. Breathing. Living. The humanness had me enamored.

TikTok brought the concepts behind static images to life.

Body positivity dominated my For You Page[26] in a matter of

---

24 The unpaid exposure a platform gives users' content. For TikTok, this mostly means video views.

25 Primarily via Megan Jayne Crabbe, whose content helped and still helps my relationship with physical movement.

26 TikTok refers to its users' main video feed as their For You Page or FYP. Based on my experiences, the TikTok algorithm seems to curate the content it puts on your FYP based on your interests, what type of content you engage with versus ignore, and who you follow.

hours. Queer content, fat-acceptance content, and self-acceptance content quickly followed. I'd never seen so much diversity on social media. No two people on my FYP looked exactly alike. People with different body types, physical features, assistive devices and technology, and personal backgrounds popped up and shared their stories, outfits, creativity, and opinions.

Body-positive content opened my eyes to so much. I learned that the implicit and explicit biases against fat people I'd witnessed and experienced had a name: fatphobia. I learned about the body positivity movement's roots in activism and advocacy for racial, LGBTQ, and fat rights and representation. I read about the fatness spectrum and different types of privilege, the commodification of body positivity, and the erasure and misrepresentations of the body positivity movement's origins. I dug deeper into every new term, movement, and concept I found. I was blown away by all the information, research, and frameworks that directly contradicted almost everything I'd ever been told about my body, about my *existence*. It gave a whole new meaning to the phrase "You don't know what you don't know" for me.

I became aware of my internalized fatphobia and ableism. I started processing and healing them. I questioned their roots. My internalized biases simultaneously made perfect sense to me and confused me.

On the one hand, growing up in a religious, southern town at an academically rigorous school as a tall, curvy girl with undiagnosed ADHD made me hate my body and brain. I felt like I couldn't do *anything* right. As if I had failed at existing. Shame consumed me every time I tried to socialize, study, work, eat, or otherwise interact with or exist in front of others. People reacted to me in a way that screamed "There is something slightly off about you, even if I can't put my finger on it." I strained to study and mimic the behaviors of those around me, but the *allegedly* correct times and ways to apply these behaviors (facial expressions, turns of phrase, vocal volume, etc.) often eluded me. I cursed my brain for missing social cues, daydreaming, and forgetting everything important, like the algebraic formula I forgot on a test because my brain decided to remember the way the classroom smelled the day I learned the formula instead of *remembering the actual formula*.

Subtext became public enemy No. 1. I hated the anxious hot flashes and knots that writhed in my stomach each time I realized someone was trying to ask or tell me something without directly asking or telling me. Sometimes I could sense when subtextual communication occurred, but rarely could I decipher its meaning or implications. Asking for clarity never ended well, either. You simply don't speak plainly in polite southern society, my dear. Everything has hidden meanings. "Bless your heart" is an insult.[27] When I tried to communicate directly, people either interpreted it as a subtextual response and doubled down on the unspoken game or they realized I genuinely had no idea what was going on and stopped talking to me. Both scenarios made me feel like a failure defined by interpersonal inadequacy.

I hated my body each time my school dress-coded me for wearing "inappropriate outfits" even though my clothes followed the rules about length, fabric thickness, and neckline. I knew the problem was the body beneath the clothes. My body. Its bigness. The same bigness that followed me into stores, changing and locker rooms, relationships, the mirror, and everywhere else I went. I couldn't hide it. I couldn't escape it. I hated it.

On the other hand, I loved the things I hated about myself when they were present in other people. My little brother and lifelong best friends have ADHD. Nothing on this earth fills my

---

27 And a warning or even a threat if someone purses their lips before they say it. If their eyebrow twitches, too, run.

heart with more joy than being with them. I watch them pace around the room when we talk, punctuate every conversational plot point with hand movements, and animate every person in their retellings of their days with funny faces and voices. I love observing how their brains work in real time. The connections they draw and patterns they see that no one else notices amaze me. The ideas they have for board and video games, beadwork, illustrations, fashion designs, band names, businesses, books, and a hundred other creations and inventions delight, thrill, and inspire me.

We communicate intuitively, in the ways that come naturally to us. When something excites them so much that they blurt it out without waiting for me to finish my sentence, I don't take offense or consider it rude. Joy overwhelms me to share in their excitement and know that we mutually understand one another. We interrupt. We go on tangents. We laugh loudly and stim as we speak. We stare at the wall as we listen. We aren't sure what our faces do mid conversation. We don't monitor or worry about our volume, body language, subtext, and the thousand other things that perplex us in other social situations. We grant each other the freedom to exist and be loved in our most natural state. I love my family and friends. I love their ADHD brains.

As for my bigness, my inability to hide, I loved that in my family members, too. My grandfather, Grampa, was the most positive and consistent male role model, father figure, and fat person in my life. Confidence, security, and strength radiated from Grampa so intensely that even I could see and understand its unspoken effect. He took up space. He took his time. He never asked anyone to wait for or listen to him. People waited and listened anyway. They chose to because they respected him. I watched it happen everywhere we went with wide, wonder-struck eyes. Grampa was big in every way. He had a big heart, a big presence, a big body, and a big impact.

Grampa's bigness didn't make me love him any less. If anything, I loved him even *more* for it. Grampa kept me safe. He often fell asleep in his recliner while watching TV. When bad dreams woke me up as a child, I'd tiptoe out into the living room and tap Grampa's hand. He'd pull me up onto his big, warm belly and tell me not to worry about the "wiseguys" in my dreams. He said he'd squash the monsters and sit on the bad guys. Bad guys aren't so scary when you picture them wriggling beneath your superhero grampa like a crushed cockroach. I'd laugh, lay my head on his chest, and sleep the rest of the night through.

Everything I hated about myself was something I adored about someone I loved. I had lists miles long of reasons why my loved ones were wonderful in every way. Why didn't my brain extend that kindness to me? Why was I an exception to the rules? Was my ongoing trauma and the culture of my childhood really enough to make me hate traits in myself that I loved in others? I wasn't sure. I accepted that I may never know exactly what combination of things planted the seeds of self-hatred within me and shifted my focus to something I could control[28]: the soil nurturing the seeds. Self-hatred still grew within me. What or who fed it, and how? What about the way I lived my life, engaged with others, and understood myself continued to reinforce my self-hatred?

I gave up on the "I'll beautify myself into self-love!" idea and swapped it for research. I gobbled up all the resources I could find. Articles, books, videos, social media captions. My

---

28 At least partially.

fascination[29] with understanding myself and those around me, perhaps born of my perceived inability to do so, permeated every waking moment. I kept reading about fat, queer, and disability advocacy. I studied the psychological definitions of self-love and self-care, compared them to the mainstream versions of self-love and self-care, and weighed the concepts against each other on my walks. I watched video essays about self-acceptance while I waited for my breakfast bagels. I listened to podcasts about ADHD, internalized misogyny, and ableism while I showered. I listened to podcasts about comorbid PTSD, depression, and anxiety while I did my skin-care routine. I watched videos about self-awareness, emotional regulation, and toxic positivity while I diced vegetables and cooked.

The more I learned, the angrier I got at just how wrong I was about everything, but I stopped directing my anger at myself. I stopped hating myself for my ill-informed perspectives.[30] I turned to the incorrect and incomplete information that informed those perspectives and placed the blame on its shoulders. I swore I'd keep tracking down new, better information. I threw everything I had into my cause. All the money I'd saved from over a decade of working and collecting scholarships. All my time. All my energy. Forget everything else, even the lifelong dreams. Forget the music. Forget the writing. Forget the art. Come hell or high water, I would find a way to be kinder to myself. No matter who else

---

29 *Hyperfixation* or *special interest* might be more accurate terms. The human experience and condition have fascinated me for as long as I can remember. When I was in preschool, started asking my mom what makes us human, where we come from, where we go when we die, and why my favorite cartoon characters allegedly didn't have human souls. I discovered all my favorite characters and people were either fictional or mortal. I wanted to save Larry the Cucumber and Steve Irwin from either fate, fictionality and mortality. I'm not exaggerating when I say I became deeply depressed when I realized I couldn't.

30 I recognize that I did the best I could with the information I had at the time. That's all I ever ask of anyone else, so I finally let that be enough for me, too.

abandoned and neglected me, I refused to abandon and neglect myself. Not again. Not this time. I'd fueled myself with stress, anxiety, spite, and self-hatred for far too long.

I steeled myself with love. *Real* love, not fleeting positive feelings. I called the parts of myself I hid and hated out into the open. I put my ideas into practice. I started posting about my journey to find and create accessible self-love and self-care systems. I didn't think twice about using my real voice, not the high-pitched version I once wore as a shield. I treated TikTok like a video journal. I launched all my thoughts, theories, trials, failures, and successes out into the digital world as I learned how to make peace with my existence. My enthusiasm for the process prospered. It sustained my self-care routines, my analysis of and work on my self-concept, and my research about the limitations of self-care and self-worth. Dormant magic—my creativity and imagination—stirred within me again. Flashes and fragments of unformed potential fluttered in and out of existence in my mind's eye. I buzzed with anticipation.

Finding My Fairy Godmother

On May 29, 2020, I stood in the bathroom waiting to undress. Water rushed forth from the showerhead. The ceiling vent droned as the air humidified around me. I quietly locked the door and removed my clothes. My fingertips hovered over the faded purple and white stretch marks that zigzagged down my chest and curled across my stomach. I exhaled and turned to the side. My lower belly curved out above my hips. Skin, fat, and muscle folded in on each other and cascaded down from my back into rolling arcs on my sides. Dimpled skin—cellulite—dotted my upper thighs. I pondered my reflection. I wasn't shaped like this three years ago, when I was still a teenager. I had never truly looked at this version of my body, this adult woman's body, before. A light layer of fog formed on the mirror. I turned forward again, and the rest of the world melted away.

It was just me and my reflection.

My shoulders dropped. I straightened my back and stood at my full height. My spine cracked as my weight shifted. I blew all the air out of my lungs. I let my stomach—*me*—relax. I stepped back. I'd looked at myself in the mirror every day for a few weeks by then, but I saw myself for the first time that day.

A strong softness surrounded me. The lines and curves that defined me flowed uninterrupted by the tension, shame, and fear I typically carried in my bones. There were parts of me I still did not know how to accept. The true extent of my bigness—my height, my weight, the space my existence demanded—intimidated me, but the fear dissolved the longer I looked at myself in this relaxed, raw state. I was big. I was tall. I was fat. I was curvy. I had body hair and stretch marks and scars and cellulite and zits and fine lines and wrinkles, but so what? None of it was bad. None of it was good, either.

It just *was*.

I stepped into the shower in this headspace. The lines of a poem[31] strung themselves together in my head as I scrubbed my scalp.

> *I am fat.*
> *Not an insult or compliment,*
> *simply a statement of fact.*

I chewed on the words and rinsed out my shampoo. I experimented with a few more.

> *I have some flab, but I don't look drab.*

---

31 This poem, entitled "I Am Fat," can be found in Part I.

I lathered soap onto my stomach. It jiggled. I smiled.

In fact, I think I look fab!

I raced through the rest of my shower. The lines just kept coming. They were short. They rhymed. They were unlike anything I'd ever written or even considered writing before. I dried my hands just enough to snatch my phone off the counter and jot everything down. Water dripped from my hair onto the floor.

I read the finished poem back to myself and grinned from ear to ear. It was perfect. Objective, but kind. No forced assurances about desirability. No comparisons between body sizes. It encouraged everyone to eat. I *loved* it. I felt like the poem was me, somehow. I dried off, wrapped myself in a towel, and bounded out into the bedroom to read it to my partner at the time. They shrugged, called it fun, and then returned to their video game. My chest flared. I tightened my towel around me, thanked them, and slunk back into the bathroom. I closed the door.

I looked at my reflection again. My shoulders were wound up to my ears. My neck craned down. My feet pointed in. I held a perpetual breath. My eyebrows shot up when it finally clicked.

The reflection staring back at me didn't feel like my poem. She didn't feel like me anymore, either. I was working so hard to take care of myself and rediscover my artistic passions, but I was still shrinking myself. Why? What was I so afraid of? I looked down at my poem and back up at my contorted reflection. The me in the mirror asked:

Are you sure you want to do this?
Are you sure you can do this?
Real art isn't fun. Real artists don't look like you.
Is your art even worth making?
Does your voice matter?

I held her gaze for a moment. Then I took a deep breath, dropped my towel, shook my shoulders out, and stretched back up to my full height. I jumped once and watched my body bounce and ripple. I laughed. I looked at myself in all my big, fat, tall, queer, ADHD, mentally ill, whimsical-poem-writing glory and said,

"I am not afraid of you. You can scream at me, run from me, make fun of me, and resist me all you want, but I am going to love you so much you won't even know what to do with it, and that's okay because I'll *teach* you what to do with it. You are not too difficult. You are not too much. You are enough. You have always been enough. We will do this together. I will stay with you. I will fight for you. I will find a way to take care of you, and if I cannot find one, I will *create* one."

And that's exactly what I did.

I stopped listening to commodified self-love and self-care narratives and made a holistic system designed by me, for me to help me consistently meet my needs. I created daily self-care routines that accommodate my lowest and highest ability and resource levels. I used a psychological foundation to devise and define my own understanding of the self.[32] I embraced new ways of living. I offered myself empathy, patience, and time to adjust when change overwhelmed me. I embraced creating. I let myself write short poems that rhymed. I let myself make music. I let myself be a beginner. Make mistakes. Learn. I leaned into creative freedom and stopped trying to make myself so small, serious, and palatable. The more I allowed myself to be me and have fun, the more people responded to my art.

On August 9, 2020, I shared a poem encouraging everyone to eat.[33] A friend of mine from high school commented and called me

---

32 I call it The Self-Worth Web. It's coming up in Chapter 2.
33 This poem, entitled "Thank You For Eating With Me," can also be found in Part I.

"the fairy godmother of TikTok." That comment bounced around in my brain the next day as I ran errands. I went to Walmart for paper towels and left with a sparkly white shawl. I walked into Target for tomatoes and walked out with butterfly hair clips. I sat down to write, and a narrative voice I hadn't heard before but recognized instantly cleared its throat and commanded my pen. Compartmentalized bits and pieces of me merged to create someone new. My background in musical theater, my interest in fantasy and magic, my public speaking skills from speech and debate, my passion for TikTok, and my life-long love affair with writing fused into the fairy godmother. I wrote the first fairy godmother poem that day and recorded it later that evening in my all-white outfit and butterfly hair clips.

I went on to write the poems in Part I and perform them as the fairy godmother, too. At some point, I stopped performing. The fairy godmother evolved from a narrative voice and magical character into a permanent part of me. I hear her voice in my head when I get scared, sad, and angry. No matter how my self-esteem fluctuates, she's always there, waving her magic wand and sprinkling fairy dust over my fears. She reminds me that she's not scared of me and that there is nowhere I could go and nothing I could do that would make her stop loving me.

I became my own fairy godmother. I showed the scared, angry parts of me fueled by anxiety, stress, and spite that they could trust me. I let myself feel all my repressed emotions without shame and without letting my feelings further fuel my self-hatred. I separated moral concepts of good and bad from my fluctuating emotional state and physical being. I found and created sustainable ways to take care of myself. I slowly but surely earned my own trust. My ability to accept myself grew. I granted my heart's deepest desire and made it safe for me to be who I am. Now, I'm here to help you find and create ways to do the same. You deserve to feel safe to be who you are. You deserve accessible, inclusive care and love.

CHAPTER 2

CONCEPTS OF THE SELF:
The Self-Worth Web

Wellness is not just a medical, metaphysical, or spiritual concept in the West. It's become a billion-dollar industry. Industrialized wellness and the commodification of self-care—treating self-care like something that can be packaged into single-use, purchasable items instead of a sustainable set of recurring actions taken to fulfill our basic needs[34]—creates consumer feedback loops within us that deplete our resources (time, money, and energy) yet still leave us feeling unfulfilled. The wellness industry then capitalizes on our feelings of unfulfillment to sell us more products by claiming that these *new* products will bring us *real* pleasure or peace. We buy the new products, and the cycle repeats.

Peace, happiness, and pleasure are states of being. They come

---

34 All humans need consistent access to food, water, air, and shelter to survive. These are your basic needs.

and go. Their permanence cannot be bought. Regardless of your state of being, your basic needs remain constant and require regular fulfillment. By design, the wellness industry urges us to make new purchases and expensive lifestyle changes to achieve temporary states of being without acknowledging that fleeting feelings, however pleasant, cannot soothe the sadness, fear or anger caused when we cannot safely, sustainably fulfill our basic needs.

Life is subjective and relative. Our resources, ability levels, cultural backgrounds, wants, and needs vary. No singular, objective approach to life exists that is accessible to and designed for everyone. There isn't one way—a daily routine, a spiritual value system, a mind-set or framework—to live that meets everyone's needs. When we engage with generalized ideas about self-love and self-care, we must remember that any resource we encounter on the best way to live can only make claims about "best" relative to the life of the creator of the resource.

I cannot and will not tell you the best way to live your life. I am not here to subject you to the vicious self-help cycle that trapped me for years. Your potential for growth and your worthiness of acceptance right now, as you are in this moment, are not mutually exclusive. You don't have to achieve a certain level of external, tangible, or measurable success to be good enough. You are already good enough. You don't need to make a million dollars, attain a specific physique, or "completely heal" to earn food, rest, and relaxation. Your right to have your basic needs met is not contingent on your productivity, performance, body, ability, identity, or progress. You aren't a product to be perfected. You don't need to implement every single one of the newest, most efficient self-help methods to be a disciplined, productive person. You aren't a machine.

You're *human*.

Your value is inherent. You deserve respect and consideration simply because you exist. You deserve to have your basic needs met, on your best and worst days and on every day in between, and that is what I am here to do: to offer you all my knowledge about the concepts, routines, and frameworks that help me meet my basic needs, maintain a secure yet flexible self-concept, and foster high self-esteem. Though I approach these concepts using psychological definitions and frameworks, I am not a scientist, mental health professional, or medical practitioner. My perspective is still just that: a subjective, personal perspective based on my lived experience. You may or may not agree with me or find my perspective valuable. That's okay! I ultimately aim to empower you to make your own decisions by exposing you to different ideas.[35]

Now, let's do something fun. Grab something you can use to write or record an idea. It can be digital or physical. You can use this page if you'd like.

I'm going to ask you a question. Ready? Okay:

When you think of yourself, what first comes to mind?

Is it a word?

An image?

A feeling?

A memory?

Write it down, but only the first thing, whatever you thought of immediately. If it's an image, name or describe it in a few words.

Look at what you wrote. Read or listen to it out loud.

How did your body physically react to hearing what you think of yourself?

---

35 Hopefully I can save you some time, too. It's taken me years to track down all this information and make my red-string bulletin board theories to figure out how it works together. If my calculations are correct, you can probably finish this book much faster than that. Maybe not. Heaven knows I either finish a book in one sitting or take my sweet time reading it. C'est la vie avec ADHD (or that is life with ADHD, for those who don't speak French).

Did your shoulders drop, tense, or rise?

Does your back hurt?

Did you sit up a little straighter?

Did your back bend a bit more?

Did you cross or uncross your legs?

Are you bouncing your leg?

Did you freeze or become rigid?

Did you sigh, smile, or relax?

Is your stomach at ease, turning, or churning?

Does your chest feel tight?

Does your head feel light?

Is your face flushed, cold, or comfortable?

Are you itchy?

How does your throat feel?

Did you physically react anywhere in your body to what you just read, even if you aren't sure how to describe your reaction? Did you physically feel something even if you don't know what, if anything, you experienced emotionally? Write or record your physical reaction alongside your first thought. If you didn't have any physical reactions that you noticed, write "none." **Keep this exercise. You'll need it later.**

You may wonder why I asked you to do this. Isn't this supposed to be a book? You're here to read, not write. And you're right! This is a book, but essays and anecdotes can only do so much. Self-exploration requires *action*.

Form your own opinions and perspectives as you read. Jot down questions you have for further research. Remember, research can be as simple as looking something up online or as complex as becoming a ghost who haunts patrons at your local library until they help you find the answers you seek. Take note of why you agree or disagree with me. Carve the word "WRONG!!!" into the page in red ink next to anything you really hate. Draw hearts around anything you really love. Draw a doodle just because you can.

This is YOUR book.

This book exists FOR YOU.

Do whatever you want with it!

Back to self-exploration and other concepts of the self. What does all that mean? There's a short answer and a long answer. The short answer is that concepts of the self are ideas, mind-sets, or frameworks we have about specific parts of who we are or what we call our self (our beings and bodies). These concepts vary in malleability. Sometimes we can shift them easily. Sometimes it takes time, practice, and patience to change them. Sometimes we aren't yet aware of the subconscious beliefs, fears, and biases within us that influence these concepts.

Self-love is just one concept of the self. There are many more. In this chapter, we'll explore self-love, self-care, self-concept, self-focus, self-regulation, self-acceptance, self-esteem, and self-worth through a handy-dandy little system I created for myself called the Self-Worth Web. As we chat about the concepts of the self that comprise the Self-Worth Web (the long answer), I'll make and develop three key points: (1) multiple, distinct concepts of the self exist; (2) you and I will understand and apply these concepts differently; (3) our goal is not perfection.

The first key point: multiple, distinct concepts of the self exist. They have different definitions, applications, and impacts on our lives. Much of modern media describes self-love as positive feelings you have about yourself. The wellness industry often claims you can create these positive feelings with superficial self-care or self-confidence: singular acts of treating yourself and faking it till you make it. Though singular acts of self-care and faking self-confidence to try and authentically facilitate it can make us feel better sometimes, it's difficult to achieve and maintain a lasting impact on our self-esteem with superficial acts and mind-sets. Singular, inconsistent actions do not alter our daily routines or ingrained behavioral patterns and the mind-sets we reinforce with them.

My biggest beefs[36] with the simplified, commodified definitions of self-love that dominate pop culture are: (1) they expect us to remain in a permanent, positive state of being even though states of being are transient, (2) they don't explain that positive feelings about ourselves actually come from high levels of self-esteem, *not* self-love, and (3) they don't explain the other concepts of the self that contribute to high levels of positive, secure self-esteem. As I learned about concepts of the self and applied what I learned to my life, I created the Self-Worth Web to understand the relationships between the individual factors and conditions that influence states of being and self-esteem.

The Self-Worth Web is a visualization of these relationships that includes definitions of each concept. The definitions featured in the Self-Worth Web are partially inspired by the American Psychological Association's online dictionary's definitions and partially created by my specific understanding of these concepts as informed by how I practice each concept. I call it a web because all the concepts interact with each other.[37] No one concept exists in isolation.

When my self-hatred flares, the Self-Worth Web helps me pinpoint where I might be struggling internally and why. My former understanding of self-love left me feeling frustrated and hopeless. Every time I felt bad or neutral, I thought I'd stopped loving myself and couldn't figure out why. Now I can assess myself

---

36 This is a colloquial way to say, "My problem with or reason to dislike this thing."

37 And because I like alliteration. "The Self-Worth Web" sounds a lot cooler than "this flowchart I made."

and my emotional state of being with more accuracy (and with the flexibility necessary to allow for negativity and neutrality, which are normal parts of the human experience). I regularly check in with my internal Self-Worth Web to maintain my self-esteem. It gives me a more complete, accurate resource to help guide me through painful experiences like loss and instability.

THE SELF-WORTH WEB

The Self-Worth Web is intended to help individuals better understand themselves. Each component of the Self-Worth Web is a form of either awareness, action, or evaluation. Self-love and self-focus are forms of awareness. Self-care and self-regulation are forms of action. Self-concept, self-acceptance, self-esteem, and self-worth are forms of evaluation. The Self-Worth Web is informed by Western psychology and limited in application. Chapter 3 addresses its structural limitations.

SELF-WORTH

Your evaluation of yourself as a valuable, capable human being deserving of respect and consideration. Positive feelings of self-worth tend to be associated with a high degree of self-acceptance and self-esteem, but self-worth can be influenced by external factors.

SELF-ACCEPTANCE

Objective/neutral assessment and recognition of your abilities, strengths, and limitations, achievements and areas for improvement, and your physical self-image.

SELF-ESTEEM

The degree of positive feelings associated with your self-concept (your physical self-image, your accomplishments and capabilities, your values and how you live up to them, and your perceived social success/how you think others view and respond to you).

SELF-CONCEPT

Your understanding, description, and evaluation of yourself, including your psychological, physical, and social characteristics, qualities, skills, values, interactions, and roles. Sometimes subconscious biases can influence your evaluation of yourself without your conscious awareness.

SELF-FOCUS

Intentionally directing conscious attention to the state of your existence (both internally and relative to others), your thoughts, your needs, your wants, and your emotions. In this context, self-focus is objective self-awareness, *NOT* self-consciousness (excessive sensitivity or concern about yourself or your interactions with others) or selfishness (only focusing on yourself and not the needs of others).

SELF-REGULATION

Controlling your behavior through self-monitoring (keeping a record of behavior), self-evaluation (assessing the information obtained during self-monitoring), and self-reinforcement (rewarding yourself for appropriate behavior or for attaining a goal).

SELF-LOVE

General awareness of and interest in your emotional, mental, and physical being and your contentment/satisfaction. Self-love is consideration of yourself, not a literal feeling of romantic love, physical attraction, infatuation, or adoration.

SELF-CARE

Actions taken to fulfill basic personal care needs (like eating, bathing, and dressing) and assist in fostering general contentment, including seeking assistance to complete personal care needs and foster general contentment.

Section I: Self-Love

Let's start with self-love and work our way through the web.

The American Psychological Association (the APA), a scientific and professional organization of psychologists in the United States, defines self-love as "regard for and interest in one's own being or contentment."[38] I interpret *being* to mean my physical, mental, emotional, and spiritual being: my body, mind, and spirit (or whatever intangible thing you believe makes us human, even if that's just consciousness). *Contentment* refers to safety, security, social support, and the fulfillment of basic and psychological needs. At its simplest, self-love is choosing to be aware of—not ignore, suppress, or avoid—yourself and your existence.

Love as an action differs from love as an emotion. Try not to think about self-love the way you think about romantic feelings or attraction. You don't have to feel *in love* with yourself to love yourself. Feeling in love with yourself can help sometimes, but it's not necessarily the kind of love we need in our daily lives. I love myself, but I don't always adore or feel *in love* with every little thing about myself, my body, and my choices. I don't have to. I deserve acknowledgement and consideration even when I make a mistake, am in a bad mood, or struggle with insecurities. So do you. You don't have to be perfect to be worthy of love. True love considers the imperfect parts of us, too, not just the parts that seem easy to celebrate. Plus, life would be awfully boring if we never did anything wrong. How would we ever learn? What stories would we share over brunch?

When you let go of the idea that self-love looks like limerent [39]

---

38 American Psychological Association. (n.d.). Self-love. In *APA Dictionary of Psychology*. Retrieved April 2023, from https://dictionary.apa.org/self-love.

39 Psychologist Dorothy Tennov coined the term "limerence" to describe the intense feelings of desire, sensitivity, and concern for a partner that can characterize the early stages of relationships or romantic obsessions.

love, you free yourself from the pressure to maintain constant feelings of passion, adoration, and intensity toward yourself, which isn't sustainable. Self-love is not forcing yourself to be happy when you're not. Self-love is not expensive skin care and bubble baths.[40] To me, self-love is simply an awareness of the state of my existence. It's an intentional interest in my well-being. It's a consideration of my needs. Of my safety. Of my emotions. Of my physicality.

> When I recognize that I am hungry, and I eat, I practice self-love.

> When I recognize that I want or need to move, and I move, I practice self-love.

> When I recognize that I want or need to rest, and I rest, I practice self-love.

> When I recognize that my desires could hurt me, and I resist them, I practice self-love.

> When I recognize desires that could fulfill me, and I indulge them, I practice self-love.

> When I consider my needs even when they contradict each other, I practice self-love.

> When I consider my needs even if I can't or won't take action to fulfill them, I practice self-love.

---

40 These things can be singular acts of self-care or parts of your daily self-care routines, which we'll discuss in more detail in the next section.

When I direct my attention to my needs even if I am unsure of what they are or how to fulfill them (for example, struggling to identify hunger), I practice self-love.

Choosing awareness over avoidance or neglect—the conscious, intentional choice to consider myself and my existence—is self-love. Self-love has grown into consideration of myself without guilt, shame, and anger for me, but that is neither a necessary component of this kind of self-love nor the way I initially practiced this kind of self-love. With this kind of self-love, you can still consider your needs even if it frustrates or embarrasses you. Therefore, you can love yourself more attainably without the burden of simultaneously fostering positive emotions.

I struggled with self-love for years before developing this framework. I thought I had to feel *in love* with myself to love myself. I considered self-love objective, not subjective. I thought everyone needed to do and think the same things to love themselves. I thought there was one answer, one self-love ring to rule them all, and that one day I'd find a magical list of everything I needed to do to finally love myself. I thought someone other than me could, would, and should author this list, that someone other than me could tell me exactly how to love myself even though they'd never lived a single second of my life.

I didn't realize that only I know the truest state of my being and existence at any given point in time. I didn't realize that only I know what brings me true contentment. I didn't understand that self-love is subjective and highly relative to YOUR needs, YOUR state of being, YOUR ability levels, and YOUR contentment.

There is no universal right or wrong way to exist. There is no singular, objective way to fulfill human needs and facilitate contentment that works for and is accessible to everyone. Every time I read an article or post about self-love, I tried to apply the information as law when I should have treated it like a suggestion. That's what this book is—a book of suggestions on how you can create a kinder relationship with yourself and information that might help you get started. Ultimately, only you choose what you find useful. Remember all those cheesy sayings about you being the "only you"? They're *true*. You are the only version of your exact self in the only version of your exact body with your exact brain at this exact point in the present in this specific timeline, universe, and reality that ever was and ever shall be.

You are the only *qualified* expert on your being and contentment.

Doctors, friends, family members, spiritual leaders, educators, mentors, and other trusted advisers can offer you their insight, guidance, and recommendations on how you ought to live, but even those recommendations rely on the data you provide to them about yourself and your experiences. Even those recommendations must first pass through those folks' internal biases and frameworks. Anyone can offer you their opinion on life, but they developed that opinion based on *their* lived experience, not yours. They're the expert on *themselves*, not on you. Keep an open mind, consider others' perspectives, but do not ever let anyone convince you that they know you, your body, or your needs better than you do, let alone how you should[41] live your life.

You are the ultimate authority on you.

You get the final say.

Before we move on to self-care and key point No. 2, I want to share something with you.

I detest contradictions. I *loathe* them. I like my communication the way I like my water: clear. Contradictions confuse me, and I

---

41 Whatever that means . . . Wait, have I done this footnote bit about the word "should" before . . . ? Hmm.

hate feeling confused. When a person's instructions, actions, or words contradict each other, I stew over every tiny detail trying to make sense of what I'm actually supposed to do with the information or take away from the interaction. I can't stand contradictions.

Unfortunately, life is full of 'em.

I will inevitably contradict myself, though that pains me to admit. There was a time that I thought I was above contradictions. I thought I could avoid them and find the one true answer to all my questions about self-love if I just researched and meditated hard enough. Clearly, that didn't happen.

Please trust that I am just as annoyed about the inevitability of contradictions as you might be, if not more so. Alas, we cannot avoid them when we talk about the human experience. To be human is to embody contradictions. On a tightrope. Over a giant canyon. Holding a baton. Opposing ideals, morals, systems, wants, needs, and values hang suspended from opposite ends of our batons. We must find a way to balance (or teeter back and forth, more realistically) as we walk the tightrope of life. As much as I wish we could just chuck the baton into the canyon and get airlifted off the tightrope, we cannot. We have to deal with contradictory concepts and figure out how to strike a balance between them.

Self-love narratives used to frustrate me because I took them and all their contradictions literally. I tried to apply all the contradicting information at once and created chaos. It maddened me. Do you know how annoying it is to try something new just to be told you're not only doing it wrong, but you should in fact be doing the complete opposite of what you're currently doing? And then to get told a few weeks later that you weren't *totally* wrong, so you should go back to what you were originally doing, but you have to change certain details of your approach because those aren't the best ways to do what you were doing anymore? *Oh*, and one last thing, you also need to throw out everything you were told to buy three weeks ago and buy this new thing if you want to love yourself the *right* way. UGH!

I felt caught between trying to have a positive attitude no matter what and allowing myself to have bad days. I wasn't sure if I had to love every inch of my body or accept my insecurities. Confusion overwhelmed me with every new self-love article I read. I'd shake my fist at the sky and shout, "All right, wise guy! Which is it?" No one ever answered. Maybe you shouldn't shake your fist at the powers that be. Who knows? The point is that multiple concepts of the self exist with unique definitions and applications. All of them can and do work together, but they are NOT all the same things. Some people treat self-love like the only and most important concept of the self, which is why so many online resources contradict each other. They say "self-love" when they mean "self-esteem," "self-worth," or "self-acceptance," and they don't bother clarifying or explaining that all these different ideas, not just self-love, contribute to our quality of life.

Don't get me wrong: quick, easily consumable resources serve an important purpose. They expose us to new ideas, perspectives, and terms. Furthermore, as a creative person limited by form and technology, too, I get it. It's hard to nestle nuance into a fifteen-second video or two-hundred-word article. However, once we progress beyond initial exposure and seek to understand and apply new concepts, frustration and confusion ensue when the most readily available resources contradict each other or don't tell us where to find more in-depth information.

People have lots of opinions about self-love. What it means. What it looks like in practice. How you behave if you do or don't have it. How you should behave if you want it. As a human with opinions of my own, I love a good opinion piece. As an author with a journalism degree, I dislike when people present opinions like facts. Just because one person says, "You don't love yourself if you have insecurities" doesn't make it true. That is their *opinion* and should be treated as such. I struggle with this almost as much as I struggle with contradictions. It took me a long time to process that facts and opinions don't carry the same weight even in subjective conversations about personal topics like self-love. It took me even longer to realize that we're allowed to prioritize *our* opinions over others' opinions in these conversations. We have to if we want to figure out what best suits our lives and our needs.

Section II: Self-Care

The terms *self-love* and *self-care* appear interchangeably in modern media. I understand why. If self-love is regard for one's own being and contentment, then taking care of yourself (i.e., meeting your being's needs) sounds like kind of the same thing. For me, self-care is a distinct extension of self-love. A small but significant difference marks when self-love evolves into self-care. Self-love is awareness. Self-care is action based on that awareness. Self-care can't occur without self-love occurring first, but they are still separate concepts, no matter how intricately intertwined.

Aside from the act of choosing to be aware of ourselves and our existence, self-love does not technically require action. This is what I meant earlier when I said, "When I consider my needs even if I cannot or will not take action to fulfill them, I practice self-love." Once we act to tend to our being—even if we act in intangible ways, like disengaging from certain trains of thought—we move from awareness to active involvement. Self-love and self-care are closely related, but there is an order of operations. Self-love, *interest in or awareness of our being*, happens first. Self-care, *action for or toward our being*, happens second.

Self-care can refer to specific, singular actions, like taking a bubble bath. It can also refer to ongoing or recurring actions that sustain our being and meet our needs, like drinking water each day. The APA defines self-care as "activities required for personal care, such as eating, dressing, or grooming, that can be managed by an individual without the assistance of others."[42] I disagree with the second half of that definition. Personal care tasks don't stop qualifying as self-care just because we need someone to assist us with their execution. By my definition of self-care (acting for or toward our being), asking someone for help completing a personal care task is still taking an action. Perhaps the act of asking for help becomes the true act of self-care in such instances.

What do you think? [43]

Oh, do you remember when I said I'd inevitably contradict myself in these conversations? Great. Here's contradiction No. 1. If you go back to the earlier examples of how I practice self-love, I *technically* included self-care in those statements. How awful, I know. Before you shake your fist at me as I shook mine at the sky, I have my reasons.[44] I structured those statements to reflect the order of operations between self-love and self-care. Look at this example:

"When I recognize that I am hungry, and I eat, I practice self-love."

---

42 American Psychological Association. (n.d.). Self-care. In *APA Dictionary of Psychology*. Retrieved April 2023, from https://dictionary.apa.org/self-care.

43 It's a bit lonely being the author. Have you noticed how often I use the verbs "chat," "talk," and "discuss" or otherwise ask you questions? That's because I like conversations (ironic as that may be given my disability). I like when ideas come alive. I want to explore these things with you in real time. I want to hear your ideas and perspectives. That's partially why I included writing prompts and told you to mark up this book. Ideally, we'd sit together and sip our beverages of choice while we muse and ponder all life's great questions. Since I cannot be everywhere all at once, this will have to do.

44 Perhaps the powers that be have their reasons, too . . . Sigh.

Self-love comes first. I take interest in my being and observe that I am hungry. Self-care follows. I act based on that observation to fulfill one of my needs: I eat.

Do you also remember when I said I have three key points to make throughout this chapter? Sensational. Here's point No. 2.

The second key point: Our opinions about concepts of the self differ because our needs, ability levels, cultural and familial backgrounds, and access to resources differ. We already dissected why our applications of self-love will be unique for all of us. Let's examine self-care.

You and I won't care for ourselves exactly the same way. That's expected and okay. It's also okay if you don't know how to take care of yourself yet or if you need help from other people, assistive devices, medication, or service animals to care for yourself. I didn't learn how to consistently care for myself until I was twenty-three years old. For reference, I'm twenty-four at the time of writing, so I do mean it literally when I say it took my whole life, *and* I'm still learning. It's okay if it takes your whole life, too. How old you are right now or how old you were when you first learned about self-care doesn't matter. What matters is that you're trying (which is true no matter how many breaks you need or how many times you stop and start over). You're doing what you can when you can. You keep trying, and *that's* what counts.

We can't control much in life aside from ourselves. If you tried, you did what you could. Be proud of yourself. Your efforts warrant recognition regardless of the outcome. Appreciating your efforts regardless of the outcome sustains the long-term pursuit of passions more than harsh self-criticism. Forces beyond our influence can heavily impact external outcomes. If we only acknowledge our efforts when we get the exact external outcome we want, we struggle to incentivize consistency. Athletes train even when they lose. Setting a new personal record deserves celebration even if you don't win the overall competition. The time and dedication required to practice a skill deserve recognition even if your mastery of the skill or the intensity or frequency of your practice fluctuates. Your efforts matter. Celebrate them.

If that feels hollow or cliché, I understand. It felt meaningless to me too until recently. The concepts of healthy, consistent love, encouragement, and self-care confused and evaded me for years. I heard people talk about them. Plenty of family and friends emphasized the importance of those concepts to me, but I rarely saw them at home. I had no idea how to practice self-care in my daily life. I felt unworthy of consistent, safe love.

My family loves me. Nonetheless, they were as unpredictable and exhausted as they were loving throughout my adolescence. My paternal grandfather died before I was born, and my paternal grandmother suffered from dementia until she passed away. My maternal grandparents—my grampa and grama—loved each other distantly. They lived in the same house, spoke respectfully to each other, and hosted us for family meals, but I rarely saw them express physical affection for one another. They sat on separate sides of the living room during the day and sometimes slept in separate rooms at night. Grampa typically got dressed for the day whether he left the house or not. Grama infamously wore pajamas on her walks around the neighborhood (and occasionally to the grocery store, a habit I picked up—to my mother's great dismay).

My mother divorced my father when I was a toddler. She got custody. Neither of them remarried. My father skipped his visitation weekends without notice sometimes. I'd sit on the porch and wait for him, convinced he would show, and fall asleep leaning against my backpack as the afternoon bled into the evening. My mother carried me inside on those nights. On his weekends, my father loved to take me and my brother to the movies almost as much as he loved attending Mass. He practiced Catholicism obsessively. He memorized dozens of daily prayers and forced his beliefs on me and my brother. Death and the threat of hell frightened him to the point of paranoia at times, but he seldom admitted fault outside of a confessional. He hated being challenged or told what to do. It enraged him, whether the challenge was real or imagined. He towered over us. His anger consumed and controlled him, and he in turn sought to control us. Disobedience, real or perceived, provoked his vocal and physical wrath. I often froze in fear at his house.

At the same time, he volunteered in our community. He donated money even when it was tight. He brought his guitar and fireworks to every summer party, and all our neighborhood friends cheered when he took us to the local pool. He brought underwater motorized scooters, water guns, Frisbees, and floaties and let everyone use them. He made up songs and stories to make us laugh. He got me my first guitar and then told me I'd never make it as a performer or writer. He never smoked. He never drank. He exercised every day. He prioritized his physical health for his entire life only to contract terminal cancer. He wept and finally told me he believed in me when he heard me sing in my last high school show. I clung to and cursed this new, bittersweet support for a few short months before he died in 2017 after fighting cancer for over four years.

He was a walking contradiction. Most people are. He was just as creative, funny, and kind as he was frightening, cruel, and cold. He said he loved me. I know he did in his own way, but he scared and saddened me. I learned to fear his conditional, inconsistent, unhealthy love.

Life exhausted my mother. She left my father with what she could carry. We moved in with Grampa and Grama and lived with them until we found a place of our own. My mother yearned to move far away from my hometown and her ex-husband, but she stayed. She sacrificed her wishes to give us a sense of stability. There is no doubt in my mind that she loves and always has loved me, rocky as our dynamic once was.

Before marrying my father, my mother traveled the world. She worked as a linguist and was a Fulbright scholar. She spoke three languages fluently and learned three more semi-fluently just for fun. She wanted to give my brother and me the world. She lacked the financial resources to grant us access to everything she wanted for us (primarily a strong education), so she got creative and made do with what she had: tenacity and intelligence. She taught Spanish and French at a local K-12 private school for over a decade so she could afford to send my brother and me there with tuition benefits.

I used to wonder who she was before she met my father. As a child and teenager, I knew her as stressed, scared, bold, and brilliant. She craved control in a world that robbed her of it, so she controlled who and what she felt she could. She needed a daily plan and a backup plan in case the original plan failed. She oscillated between expecting excellence and accepting our best efforts in school and at home. She got to define what "our best" meant. I learned *my* best was not always *enough*, though I did my best to follow her rules. I didn't drink or do drugs. I worked each summer and made the honor roll each semester. She spoke proudly of my achievements and loudly of my shortcomings, often on the house phone in the living room.

She communicated by screaming, sometimes for hours at a time, but she wouldn't let me walk away without a hug. She picked me up immediately when I needed her. She sprinkled cinnamon sugar on sliced bananas each summer morning in 2013 and left them under my door when I struggled to eat after my friend died in a plane crash. She designed plans for every dream I ever had and spreadsheets for every college and scholarship that piqued my interest. She attended or volunteered for all my plays and shows no matter the importance of my role. She was dedicated, involved, overworked, underpaid, and raising two children on her own. It took everything she had, especially after Grampa and Grama died while I was in high school. She urged us to take care of ourselves and our spaces but struggled to teach us how to do so or lead by example. I learned that taking care of yourself means making yourself presentable for other people. It wasn't something you did for yourself, and it didn't matter what things looked like at home.

My mom and I have a great relationship now. She changed careers in 2018, left my hometown, and moved out of the country. Her new job challenges, inspires, and supports her. I've never seen her happier or more fulfilled. She takes better care of herself, and it shows. She smiles more. She laughs louder. Her shoulders relax when she exhales. She isn't holding a perpetual breath waiting for the other shoe to drop. Every now and then, when her eyes *really* sparkle, I get a glimpse of who she must have been before, and I grin. She pursues her dreams and helps me pursue mine. We glow with pride, gratitude, and love for each other.

Despite the improvement in my familial dynamics, the profound impact of what I learned and didn't learn about love and self-care as a child and teenager remains. Still, I'm privileged and lucky that my parents verbally encouraged self-care and provided the basic building blocks for it, even if they struggled to demonstrate it. I knew I had to shower, eat, brush my teeth, and comb my hair, but I thought I only had to do all that when I left the house. Sometimes not even then. I skipped multiple meals a day; wore months-old, stained, dirty clothes; went weeks without showering; and let my hair tangle nearly to the point of matting. I thought that was okay as long as no one outside the family knew about it. I thought I was caring for myself as much as anybody else was as long as

I kept myself presentable enough to avoid affronting the outside world. I had no idea people lived any differently than that. Shock consumed me when one of my high school classmates told me she showered twice a day, every day. *Twice . . . A DAY!!*

Mental health and medical conditions complicate almost everything, including self-care. I lived and still live with depression, anxiety, ADHD, and PTSD. I knew I had various diagnoses when I was younger, but I didn't really understand them. I didn't know how my conditions impacted my levels of ability, my mindsets, my daily habits (or lack thereof), my goals, my hobbies, and my relationships. I didn't know depression can manifest as apathy, isolation, and existential despair. It isn't always literal sadness. I didn't know PTSD can look like freezing, avoidance, detaching, dissociating, hypervigilance, persecutory delusions, and insomnia. It isn't only nightmares and waking flashbacks. I didn't even know I had ADHD until right before I left for college. I had no clue how all these conditions impacted each other and my life collectively.

The mentally ill melting pot in my brain turned allegedly simple self-care tasks into herculean feats. Do you know how much mental and physical strength it takes to drag yourself away from a book when you're hyperfixated on reading it, you see no point in leaving your bed because nothing *really* matters, you can't move because the floorboards creaked outside your room earlier so now you're frozen and the low hum of the ceiling fan sounds weirdly far away, and your stomach hurts because you just *know* that something awful will happen if you leave your room even though you aren't sure exactly what? All the while, it looks to the outside world like you're just reading a book with your eyes glazed over. The strength and energy required to remobilize yourself, set your book down, and leave your room to care for yourself under these conditions quadruples when you consider that the environment and tools you need to care for yourself (like a kitchen, an egg, and a frying pan, for example, if you want to eat) potentially require you to face someone or something you actively fear. Sometimes I just didn't have it in me.

Mental illness, ADHD, and lack of self-care joined forces to trap me in a petty paradox throughout high school and college, particularly as I grieved the losses of loved ones and friends. Trying to care for myself overwhelmed me and required energy and motivation I lacked, but my mental health symptoms worsened when my needs went unmet, which drained me more.

I escaped the paradox a few months ago when I shifted my perspective on self-care tasks. I experimented with a few frameworks before I found one that worked for me. First, I consulted the professionals. I made a list of the "bare minimum" self-care tasks I should repeat daily to fulfill my physical needs, according to my doctor and therapist. I also added some items based on my emotional, mental, and spiritual needs (like spending time outside and reading). This kind of list will look a bit different for everyone depending on your needs. This is my list:

Marisa's Daily Self-Care Tasks (New & Professionally Improved/Approved!)

1. Take a.m. medicine immediately upon waking up.

2. Eat at least two meals.
    a. Try to eat at least one fruit, one vegetable, one protein source, and one carbohydrate source by the end of the day.
    b. A meal does not have to be cooked or complicated to be a meal.

3. Drink water, minimum sixty-four ounces.

4. Brush teeth twice, ideally eight hours apart.[45]

5. Shower or at least wash your face.
   a. Do not go more than four days without showering. This triggers your depression. Take a shower every other day if you can, even if it's just a five-minute shower.

6. Moisturize skin.

7. Detangle hair.

8. Move (any intensity level) for twenty uninterrupted minutes.

9. Spend at least twenty uninterrupted minutes **not** looking at a screen.

10. Read for thirty minutes.

11. Spend at least ten minutes outside, if the weather permits it.
    a. You can combine this with your twenty minutes of movement or thirty minutes of reading. Go for walks or read outside.

12. As safely as possible, talk to one other human being for at least five minutes.

13. Sleep for at least seven hours, ideally eight.

---

45 I struggle with this task to this day. It's so hard to remember.

My list intimidated and angered me at first. I'm no mathematician, but sources say that's a thirteen-item list. Some items have subtasks, too. How and where would I find the motivation and time to complete all those tasks every single day? Tasks eight through twelve alone require over an HOUR. Forget about task thirteen.[46] I felt ridiculous and selfish even thinking about spending so much time on myself. Shouldn't I spend my time on other, more important things, like helping people who actually need and deserve it? Shouldn't I be working? Generating income? Driving? Pursuing my passions? Driving some more? (I drive a lot. It takes forever to walk anywhere in my town. I'm side-eyeing you, Henry Ford, and your lobbying efforts for roads instead of walkable cities.)

Up until the conception of my new and improved list, I viewed self-love and self-care as luxuries, not necessities. The idea that I *needed* to take care of myself in order to function seemed absurd. Who did I think I was? I could survive without all this self-care crap. Who needs consistency? Security? I survived without that stuff before, so obviously I could do it again. Sure, I wanted to feel better about myself and generally experience a more peaceful, safe, and fulfilling existence, but not if it meant sacrificing efficiency![47]

I would've rather spent the day hating myself and working than caring for myself if caring for myself required setting

---

46 Rest was tough for me. At first, I tricked my brain into viewing self-care tasks as "hacks" to make me more productive, but rest took too much time away from productivity. I couldn't justify it. I've progressed a lot in healing this weird capitalist complex against rest, but in case anyone needs a reminder, REST IS SELF-CARE AND NECESSARY FOR SURVIVAL. Also, there are many kinds of rest (physical rest, social rest, sensory rest, mental rest, etc.), not just sleep. Humans need all of them. If you really can't get rid of the "but I should be working" thoughts, remember that you can't work nearly as effectively when you're not well rested. You need rest. Yes, you. Don't make me come over there with a soothing beverage and a warm blanket. Rest.

47 I blame late-stage capitalism for that mind-set, too.

boundaries to protect my time. The idea of prioritizing myself disgusted me. I didn't want to do it. It felt wrong. It went against everything I'd been taught, and I felt like I wouldn't be able to remember how and when to do it all even if I tried.[48] I would have tossed my list atop my pile of abandoned projects and called it a day for it not being coauthored and approved by professionals. When you grow up in classist academic meritocracies, you view accredited and qualified experts almost like Greek gods. They reign down from Mount Olympus, the top of the scholastic food chain. Their peer-reviewed word is law.

You do *not* throw away their recommendations.

I begrudgingly returned to my list. I couldn't shame, guilt, or hate myself into learning and implementing new ways of life. I knew I needed to shift my mind-set to turn self-care tasks into daily routines, so I used my mom's favorite problem-solving approach: I made a plan. My plan's beauty lay in its simplicity. First, I'd convince my brain to stop resisting change by finding a framework that incentivized these specific changes. Then I'd implement the changes until they became routines. [49] Easy-peasy.

The internet loves to preach about making self-care "fun." I tried turning showering and brushing my teeth into fun activities instead of useless, time-wasting chores. It didn't work. My preconceived notions about self-care being an indulgence and a luxury made the "fun" method ineffective. I was already reluctant to spend time on this stuff when I viewed it as the doctor's orders. Viewing it as "fun" landed me right back where I started: feeling

---

48 Maybe, just maybe, capitalism is not entirely to blame for this. It's possible that ADHD also played a part in it.

49 My ADHD makes it difficult, dare I say impossible, for me to create true habits (tasks you complete every day automatically/without thinking about them/ without some degree of conscious effort), so I set routines as my goal.

guilty and ashamed that I had needs and selfish for "indulging" by trying to fulfill my needs.

The "fun" approach also clashed with my mental illness melting pot. I couldn't make self-care consistently fun, and I couldn't make fun consistently incentivizing. Fun was not a necessity and therefore not worth my limited energy when depressed.

The game-changing mind-set for me considers self-care tasks neutral necessities that assist us in improving our quality of life.[50] They aren't extra chores and inconveniences we must suffer through for the sake of others. They also aren't superficial luxuries that we don't deserve or have time to indulge. They're tools—morally neutral, necessary tasks that make existing a little easier.

When I thought about showers in the past, I thought about them in extremes. I simultaneously believed that showering was a burden and a luxury, that it wasn't for me and that it was too much for me. Previously, I showered for one of two reasons. I showered when the sensory distress caused by sweat or dead skin overwhelmed me, and I showered to avoid affronting other people with my odor. I took lengthy showers (or what I once called "deep cleans") because I showered so infrequently. These deep cleans drained me. They often took the last of the executive function skills and energy I had left for the day. On this end of the extreme, showering felt like a burden because of the intention behind the action (making myself palatable for others, which reinforced the idea that I was inherently unpalatable and needed

---

50 You deserve to experience ease. You are not selfish or ungrateful for desiring a better quality of life. The same can be said about the fun approach. We are not selfish for desiring fun. However, viewing self-care as a neutral necessity made it easier for me to practice self-care guilt-free than the fun approach. Use whatever framework makes self-care the most accessible to you (whether it's one of these or something else).

to mask it) and the amount of energy it required. I avoided my reflection back then, especially before showering. I hated being confronted with my body and the physical impact of neglecting it.

As much as I loathed and procrastinated showering, as much as it drained me in the moment, nothing compared to the freshness, the newness, the physical and emotional cleanse of a deep clean. Deep cleans lifted my spirits. Even if only for a moment, they eased the perpetual internal uncleanliness that haunted me emotionally. I hardly recognized myself when I caught a glimpse of my reflection right after a deep clean. The exhausted girl with visible layers of grime coating her skin, hair, and clothes disappeared. A shiny new girl with bright eyes and rosy cheeks replaced her. On this end of the extreme, showering felt luxurious. It gave me hope. It renewed me. And because it brought me joy and took time away from my day that could have been devoted to schoolwork or employment, more than anything, it made me feel guilty, selfish, and ashamed.

I'm learning how to care for myself sustainably now, as an adult. Showering, brushing my teeth, and other daily self-care tasks are neither superfluous indulgences nor bothersome burdens. They are simply necessary tasks I complete to the degree I am able to each day to make existing a little easier. I am not selfish for desiring an easier existence or wanting to feel hopeful, new, and clean. Neither are you.

Let me emphasize *to the degree I am able to*. That's a crucial part of this approach. Some days you might not have the time, energy, or other resources to complete your daily self-care tasks. Sometimes you've got to prioritize and rearrange. For example, when I worked two back-to-back twelve-hour days recently, I knew I wouldn't have time to complete self-care tasks No. 6, No. 10, and No. 13 on my list both days in a row. Instead of judging or punishing myself for this, I acknowledged that there are only twenty-four hours in a day and pushed those three items to my next day off. Your available time and energy fluctuate. This is an inevitability no matter who you are, not a personal or moral failing. Twenty-four hours is not always enough time to do everything you aspire to do in a day, including certain self-care tasks. You're a human being doing your best. You do what you can with the resources and energy you have.

Basing self-care routines on my lowest resource and ability levels was also a game changer. "Marisa's Daily Self-Care Tasks" technically contains *daily* in the title, but there are some days that I can't do any of it. When my mental health really tanks, there are some *weeks* when I lack the energy for anything. I accommodate myself during such times by finding easier ways to care for myself (like using wipes to remove sweat from my body so I can still feel somewhat clean, eating cereal or other prepackaged foods to ensure that I still eat, letting myself sit down for tasks that I normally do standing [like cooking or cleaning] so I don't physically exhaust myself, etc.). These substitutions allow me to care for myself without the rigidity that so often led me to give up and neglect my needs in the past. Now I understand that just because I had the time and energy to do something one day does not mean I'll have the time and energy to do it the same way (or at all) the next day, and that's okay. Self-love and self-care are not all or nothing. You give what you can when you can.

Once I shifted how I view self-care to accommodate my resources and needs, completing my daily self-care tasks gradually grew easier. I resisted the change at first. I understand why my brain and body craved and found comfort in my old avoidant, neglectful self-care routines. My nervous system considered those familiar routines tried and true. They sustained my existence while I lived through trauma. Those routines, however flawed, got me through the hardest times and most hostile environments of my life thus far.[51]

It's exceedingly difficult to assess your basic needs when you're living in active, ongoing trauma. Forget about *tending* to those needs. I sometimes wonder what life would be like if I were born into different circumstances. I wonder how my mind might work. I wonder how my body, or nervous and adrenal systems, might function. I mourn the loss of my untraumatized potential. I think most traumatized people do, too, to an extent.

I try not to get lost in these thoughts anymore. I cannot change the past, as much as I wish I could. Ruminating on it only forces me to relive it instead of living presently in my current reality. Don't get it twisted; I don't ignore or suppress my trauma. To the extent that my conscious and unconscious minds allow, I let myself feel lingering rage, terror, disgust, anguish, grief, regret, and sorrow as they make themselves known to me. Sometimes they arrive in whispers. Sometimes they crash into me in waves and flood my eyes, nose, and mouth. Sometimes they bubble up from the pit of my stomach until I vomit them forth. I better understand self-regulation now. I physically feel these emotions instead of intellectualizing them, though part of me still hopes I'll find answers one day for the quiet "But why?" that burns in my bones.

As much as I can, I embrace the inherent contradiction of accepting the unchangeable past and accepting my emotions, particularly my anger. My anger demands justice. She—the angry part of me—doesn't know how to let go of certain things yet,

---

51 Hopefully I can end that sentence after "life" by the time I'm an old lady. What a fun thought: you and I as old folks. I never used to think I'd experience old age. I actually picture myself living past thirty now. I wonder what you'll look like with gray hair, my dear. I wonder what I'll look like! Do you think we'll go bald? If we do, can we get matching wigs?

and I don't know if she ever will. I accept that now. I honor my anger's existence. She is not scary or bad, especially now that I can self-regulate when she shows up instead of acting on her without processing first, even if that means simply separating myself from the world however I can when anger overwhelms me. I don't try to rid myself of her anymore. I give the angry part of me the space and time she needs to grieve her stolen innocence and autonomy and to mourn the losses of those she loved.

I know only the conscious half of the burden my body and brain shouldered to get me here. I can't even fathom its full weight. I don't think I'd want to know it even if I could. I thank my body and brain for carrying me through it all. I thank them for getting me out of unsafe environments, the places I fled consciously and the places my body violently rejected until I had no choice but to leave. I thank my body and brain for doing what they had to do to see me through to safety. I know they did the best they could with what they had.

Humans can survive harsh conditions for extended periods of time, but just because we can doesn't mean we should or must. When my body and brain resist change, I gently remind them that they did it. We're safe now. I show them the new floor beneath my feet, the roof over my head, and the photos of my friends, true friends, that line the walls. I breathe in the kitchen air, rich with the scent of seasonings and sounds of laughter that light up my home instead of screams, heavy footfalls, and sinister silence. When my body and brain crave the old routines, I show them that we do not live in the old conditions. I take my inner child's and teenager's hands. Together, we tiptoe upstairs to the shower. I show them the clean tiles, the fresh towels, and the bright lights. I show them the lock on the bathroom door. We head back downstairs, into a bedroom—*my* bedroom, where I sleep alone on my own bed. I show them the lock on my door.

85

They lock and shake it until they believe me when I tell them we are safe.

It takes time and reinforcement for us to internalize feelings of unsafety and unease. Showing yourself—giving yourself physical proof—that you are safer now or are capable of working toward future safety takes time and reinforcement, too. Try not to blame yourself if you resist changes you know will benefit you, like implementing daily self-care routines. Your body and brain might just be doing what they think they should to protect you, as frustrating as that may be.

Guilt and shame are tough to soothe, especially when you feel like your mere existence is wrong, embarrassing, selfish, or bad. In my experience, these feelings decrease the more you sit with them and perform self-care tasks anyway instead of letting these emotions convince you not to care for yourself. This is why I keep saying, "You're trying, and you're doing a good job," and encouraging progress over perfection. The expectation that self-care will be easy and feel good right away is unrealistic and even harmful for many of us. We are allowed to learn. We are *practicing* how to care for ourselves, and we are allowed flexibility for change and accommodations based on our abilities, resources, and emotional reactions to the new skills, tasks, and routines we employ.

Practicing self-care without resistance, shame, anxiety, and guilt was a big adjustment for me.[52] I showered more. I didn't have to answer to anyone except myself about the water bill or the hot water running cold. I stopped needing as many deep cleans once I showered regularly, which created the most magical but

---

52 These emotions still flare when I care for myself every now and then. For the most part, it's much easier for me to care for myself without extreme emotional reactions or resistance now that I've had a few years to practice and work through my self-hatred and trauma.

insufferably ironic domino effect. I once thought showering took too much time and energy, but the more I showered, the less time and energy each shower took, which made it easier for me to mentally convince myself to shower again the next day. I still huff and puff and drag my feet about showering sometimes, but it happens less and less. I know now that I will feel better (or at least cleaner) once I shower. The more I shower, the more I feel clean on a consistent basis (which I've discovered is quite important to me regardless of whether or not anyone else cares about my hygiene—who would've thought?). I am caring for myself for my sake, and I do so free from fear, guilt, and shame.

I wonder sometimes if this is what people mean when they say, "You have to love yourself before you can love someone else." If it is, my previously listed complaints about generalizing self-love still stand. If I were Martin Luther, I'd print this book out and nail it to the self-love industry's door. *Love* is not an accurate word or complete picture. There are a bajillion steps that went into me learning how to care for myself on a daily basis.[53] Loving myself is only one of those steps, and self-love is only one of several kinds of love that humans need. Love from friends and family, love from community matters just as much as self-love. Self-love and social support are not mutually exclusive, nor is one more or less important than the other. They work together to help us grow. We can learn about self-love from our communities and interpersonal relationships, and we can learn about interpersonal love by practicing self-love, but I digress.

We inherit our genetics. We inherit beliefs and learned behaviors about love, self-love, and self-care. We unintentionally treat opinions like facts. We absorb information from all around us and

---

53 Okay, maybe not that many, but a lot.

internalize what we see, hear, and read. We do our best with the information we have, but sometimes that information isn't what we need.

There's no way for me to know what information you have about self-love and self-care right now. You could have an amazing foundation and healthy, consistent examples of love, personal care, and hygienic practices in your life. Or your background could be a little like mine. Maybe a lot like mine. Maybe worse than mine. I simply don't know. Because I don't know, it's more efficient for me to approach this process as if you were a blank slate. Not like you're *totally* blank. Please don't factory reset yourself. I bet you've got some great party jokes, and I'd hate for you to forget those. I mean specifically in relation to information about concepts of the self.

It may be easier for you to learn how to love and care for yourself if you start by unlearning what you previously knew and finding a new framework that helps you perform self-care tasks with less resistance. It might not. This is one of those pesky times when you don't have to take my instructions literally. Use your best judgment. Check in with yourself as you progress through this book and life. Take note of how you react to new information. It's up to you to choose what to ignore, consider, or test.

Learning how to love and care for yourself takes time. It can feel strange, selfish, or even silly at first. It's not something that you can or will ever perfect, which leads me to the third and final key point: don't let the impossibility of perfection scare or dishearten you.

The third key point: Perfection is not the goal.

You are not a project or product to be perfected. Even if you treated yourself as such and somehow achieved perfection in all the areas of your life, that perfection would not be sustainable. Forces beyond our control can alter our lives in an instant. We can lose or gain everything that matters to us. We can also change our minds. What we once thought was perfect may bore us one day, and that's okay. The unending pursuit of perfection leads to burnout and stagnation. You are allowed to progress, grow, and change. You are allowed to regress or take breaks. You are allowed to make mistakes and learn. You do not have to be perfect, and you do not have to create perfect outcomes. No such things exist.

You love yourself when you take interest in your own being and contentment. You care for yourself when you act based on that interest. There is no way to perfectly love or care for yourself, because what you can give of yourself and your resources changes each day. Your time, money, and energy levels limit what you can achieve in a day, both generally and specifically in reference to self-care. Self-love and self-care aren't about achieving perfection. As long as you are trying to consider your being and contentment, you are loving yourself. Therefore, you have self-love by definition.

If you're like me, my dear, you might be wondering:

"If perfection isn't the goal . . . what is?"

The answer varies. It depends on who you ask. Some people make existence their goal, just getting from one day to the next. Some people chase power. Some people build wealth. Some people live for love. Some people make the pursuit of different goals their overarching goal. They move from fascination to fascination, eager to learn, apply, and master new knowledge and skills. Since you're reading my book, I'll give you my answer. I believe we each define the goal for ourselves.[54]

---

54 If you said or thought, "Then couldn't perfection technically be the goal?" just know you'd *technically* be right. *Technically.* But you know what you're doing, you semantic smarty-pants. I can't blame you. I do it, too. It's kind of fun, don't you think? Anyway, perfection isn't sustainable. Don't make it your goal. Or do. The choice is yours.

Section III: Self-Concept, Self-Focus & Self-Regulation

Popular self-love narratives often treat self-care like the precursor to self-love and conflate self-love with positive feelings about yourself. The problem with jumping from self-care to "positive feelings" lies in the incomplete nature of the cause-and-effect sequence it presents, which led to unsustainable and unfulfilling self-care practices for me. Defining self-love as general positive feelings about the self and approaching self-care as the precursor to these feelings not only doesn't fit the APA's definitions of self-care and self-love, but it also directly cannibalizes the APA's definition of self-esteem. Merging self-love and self-esteem into one concept and treating self-care like a set of finite actions you must complete to achieve this flawed, merged concept creates unrealistic collective expectations about what self-love and self-care can accomplish. These expectations imply that anyone who can't achieve and remain in a positive, confident state of being is failing at self-care in some way. Approaching self-care like this creates ample opportunity for feelings of shame, guilt, frustration, and inadequacy, which ultimately fueled my self-hatred. This approach also turns self-love into a fragile state of being, into something that can be gained or lost as opposed to something that can be consistently but flexibly accessed.

Understanding self-love as awareness of our being and interest in our contentment minimizes the possibility of self-love becoming something we can lose. The surety, simplicity, and security of this dynamic make self-love more accessible, which keeps it from eroding into ironic fuel for self-hatred. Even in our worst and darkest hours, many of us still mentally urge ourselves to try and tend to our needs (eat the corner of a stale cracker, take a single sip of water, etc.). The fact that we consider our needs, whether we act to fulfill them or not, is self-love according to my interpretation of the APA's definition.

Positive feelings toward the self are much more susceptible to external influence than a general awareness or consideration of the self. When someone experiences the loss or depletion of positive feelings toward themselves, they may think they have lost the ability to love themselves if they only understand self-love as positive feelings. As a result, they might double down on self-care, expecting it to make them feel the love again (to make their positive feelings return), but self-care is not the only factor that impacts these positive feelings. According to the APA,[55] these positive feelings correlate to self-worth and self-esteem, not self-love, and they are only *components* of self-worth and self-esteem, which are reliant on multiple concepts of the self and informed primarily by our self-concept. Maintaining secure self-esteem requires a conscious, intentional understanding of our self-concept and what influences it. Hence the creation of the Self-Worth Web.

Wait, aren't we talking about concepts of the self? What is self-concept? Are they the same thing?

Good question. They are not the same, though they sound quite similar.

I use the phrase *concepts of the self* as a quick, catchall way to refer to all the ideas, mind-sets, and frameworks we have about specific parts of who we are or what we call our self (our beings and bodies). Self-concept is a specific concept of the self. According to the APA, your self-concept is your "description and evaluation of [yourself], including psychological and physical characteristics, qualities, skills, roles and so forth."[56] Individual concepts of the self (such as self-love, self-care, self-focus, and self-regulation)

---

55 Also according to me because I agree with them, but they are the credible source here; I'm just the gal with the magic wand.
56 American Psychological Association. (n.d.). Self-concept. In *APA Dictionary of Psychology*. Retrieved April 2023, from https://dictionary.apa.org/self-concept.

help create and inform your self-concept. Think of concepts of the self like a factory and self-concept like one of the factory's final products. Many different parts of the factory work together to assemble the final product. Self-concept (the final product) is your holistic assessment of who you are, what your body looks like and can do, the social and personal roles and positions you occupy, your responsibilities and ability to fulfill them, your values, your skills, your interests, and your defining traits.

Self-concept sits at the center of the Self-Worth Web. All the other concepts of the self contribute to and/or rely on self-concept. Importantly, your self-concept is not concrete or objective. Your physical, psychological, and personality traits evolve and change. Your values, communities, and environments change, too, meaning how you evaluate and describe your traits will change as you and your life change. You can describe or evaluate your traits positively, negatively, or neutrally, but your self-concept will still be subjective because only you can access all the information required to form it, meaning the information is subject to biases and relative assessments of value that you may or may not consciously recognize.[57]

Self-love and self-care contribute to our self-concept by providing the foundations of awareness and action. The remaining concepts in the Self-Worth Web expand on these basic building blocks. Self-love and self-care approach awareness of and action for ourselves from broad, general perspectives. Self-focus, self-regulation, self-acceptance, and self-esteem interact with specific

---

57 In this context, *relative* means that there is no universal, objective standard to determine the value or significance of certain traits. For example, some cultures consider physical strength more valuable than creative capacity, but that does not mean physical strength is inherently more valuable than creative capacity. That determination is relative to that culture.

elements of who we are, what we do, and how we evaluate ourselves before we ultimately consider our self-worth.

Think of true self-worth like a five-hundred-piece puzzle and the media's version of self-love like a children's shape sorting toy. Sure, we can drop a block, ball, and triangle on top of our five-hundred-piece puzzle, but that isn't going to solve it. It's a false, superficial way to cover up the unsolved puzzle that remains underneath. The only way to actually solve the puzzle and get an accurate picture of self-worth is to locate the intricate puzzle pieces and figure out how to arrange them together.

We already pieced self-love and self-care together. Self-love is awareness of our being and interest in our contentment, and self-care is taking action to fulfill our needs. Self-focus and self-regulation, more targeted variants of self-love and self-care, are the next pieces of the puzzle. The APA defines self-focus as "the direction of conscious attention on oneself and one's thoughts, needs, desires, and emotions"[58] and self-regulation as "controlling your behavior through self-monitoring (keeping a record of behavior), self-evaluation (assessing the information obtained during self-monitoring), and self-reinforcement (rewarding yourself for appropriate behavior or for attaining a goal)."[59]

Self-focus resembles mindfulness and meditation to me, but not necessarily in a spiritual sense. We practice self-focus when we intentionally observe and pay attention to our thoughts and feelings. For example, let's say that your friend steals your favorite dessert off your plate without asking. You experience an emotion

---

58 American Psychological Association. (n.d.). Self-focus. In *APA Dictionary of Psychology*. Retrieved April 2023, from https://dictionary.apa.org/self-focus.
59 American Psychological Association. (n.d.). Self-regulation. In *APA Dictionary of Psychology*. Retrieved April 2023, from https://dictionary.apa.org/self-regulation.

as a result. You pay attention to the emotion even after you gain an initial awareness of it. You focus on any thoughts that arise alongside the emotion and the details that surround it (its cause, intensity, duration, etc.). You consciously observe your thoughts and feelings, no matter how fleetingly, in a deeper way than a general awareness of their existence. Thus, you practice self-focus.

Self-regulation, specifically emotional regulation in this case, takes that process a few steps farther. Say you're in the same scenario. Your friend snatches your dessert again (the scoundrel). How could they be so selfish?! You practice self-focus, observe anger growing within you, and realize you're about to lose it. That's where self-regulation, and specifically emotional regulation, comes in. You're about to blow up at your friend, but you pause and consider your record of behavior. Have you stolen your friend's dessert recently? Do you get angry at this friend often? When was the last time you told this friend to stop stealing your dessert? Next, you assess your data. You realize you and your friend actually *haven't* discussed food boundaries. In fact, your friend gave you some of their dessert last week. Oh, and you raised your voice (just a tiny bit) at your friend two days ago for something minor. They listened to you, and you two worked it out, but they did ask you to refrain from getting loud with them in the future, even if that means you need to take some time for yourself.

After you process all this, you take a deep breath and stand up. Yeah, you're annoyed about the dessert debacle, but you don't want to yell at your friend over this. It seems like they meant no harm. This should be a conversation, not a fight, and for it to be a conversation, you need to cool off. You stopped yourself from reacting immediately, and now you're allowing yourself time to process your thoughts and feelings before you respond. You excuse yourself to the restroom and take a minute to calm down. Once you feel ready, you go back to your table and politely ask your friend if they could ask first before taking your dessert in the future. Your friend agrees, apologizes, and confirms that they didn't mean any harm. They just weren't thinking. You both laugh it off. All is well.

Finally, you acknowledge how well you handled that situation. You honored your friend's boundary. You set your own boundary. You considered your record of behavior, the data you can draw from it, and your friend's well-being. You assessed your emotions, regulated yourself, considered your well-being, took an appropriate course of action, and prevented further conflict. Give yourself a hand! Seriously. You're learning a new skill. A vital part of that process is REWARDING yourself for behavioral patterns you want to reinforce. Now, rewarding yourself for a job well done does not mean you should punish yourself every time you make a mistake. Accountability is important, but self-loathing isn't helpful. Changed behavior impacts your life much more than ruminating in remorse and stewing in self-hatred. When we make mistakes, we take responsibility for our actions, apologize if necessary,[60] decide how we will change our behavior going forward, and hold ourselves accountable to

---

60 Two important notes here. No. 1: Whether it's born of malice, misunderstandings, or miscommunications, sometimes people accuse us of things we didn't do. We are under no obligation to apologize in such instances. No. 2: Not every mistake requires an apology. Sometimes you can resolve minor miscommunications with a conversation. In addition to actively listening and communicating with others, you can use your intuition, best judgment, and context clues to discern when an apology is necessary. If it is, don't be afraid. Trauma sometimes distorts apologizing into a perceived admittance of guilt and consequently something that could endanger us. However, taking accountability or communicating your feelings in an open, honest, direct way when it is safe to do so is not a sign of weakness or something to be feared. Apologizing gets easier with practice, as does detecting when an apology is necessary from or for you. You deserve apologies when you're hurt, too.

make those changes. We do what we can to make it right, and we let go.

Remember, this new skill (self-regulation) can't technically be mastered. Sometimes we feed emotions we wish we'd ignored. Sometimes we ignore emotions we wish we'd addressed. Anger used to overwhelm me. I hated myself for it because I couldn't regulate it. Wrath boiled and bubbled within me like lava in an active volcano. When something sent me over the edge, I erupted. I could feel the lava rising and threatening to destroy me if I didn't get it out. So I'd rant to anyone who would listen. I'd shout or say unkind, reactive things, which I'd then deeply regret, but I didn't know what else to do. I just wanted the pain, frustration, and fear to go away.

Self-focus and self-regulation helped me learn how to approach my anger. When I first started working on these concepts, I couldn't stop my anger if something strong enough triggered it. I used self-focus to learn how to identify the warning signs of an eruption instead. If I felt that familiar heat swelter, I'd excuse myself to any environment other than the environment that triggered the reaction until I calmed down enough to reengage (or decided against reengaging). Over time, my ability to prevent angry outbursts increased the more I practiced self-care. It's much easier to regulate when you aren't also starving, dehydrated, sleep-deprived, and overstimulated. Who knew?

Inability to achieve constant emotional regulation is not a moral failing, especially for people with PTSD, ADHD, autism, or other conditions or disabilities that make self-regulation challenging. The circumstances of our births and the physiological composition of our brains and bodies (nurture and nature) impact our proclivity for self-regulation. Many of us don't learn how to identify our emotional states, let alone how to regulate them, until well into adulthood because it wasn't safe for us to do so before. It's taken me years to learn how to self-regulate as an adult, to learn what I didn't learn as a child and teenager, to desperately try and make up for lost time, and my emotions still occasionally overwhelm me. If that describes you, too, you're not alone. We must be patient with and compassionate toward ourselves. We are trying now, when we can, as we learn how to live with the weight of things we may not even fully remember. That takes strength. It takes time. You are here, you are trying, and that is enough. You are doing a good job.

Our thoughts and emotions are ultimately information. We decide what we want to do with that information. Do we want to act based on it? Do we want to ignore it? Do we want to challenge it or seek help for it if it overwhelms us? Do we want to lean into it and feel it more deeply? You're not a bad person for experiencing and expressing negative emotions. Grief, anger, sadness, disappointment, jealousy, and so forth are all part of the human experience. Practice self-focus and self-regulation. Do your best to discern whether an emotion warrants action. Reward yourself for behavioral patterns you want to reinforce and hold yourself accountable without excessive self-loathing when you make mistakes. Take the patience and compassion you offer others and extend it to yourself as well. We're all learning. We're all human.

Section IV: Self-Acceptance & Self-Esteem

Self-acceptance and self-esteem evaluate your self-concept. Self-acceptance is an objective overview of the various qualities that comprise your self-concept. The APA defines self-acceptance as "a relatively objective sense or recognition of one's abilities and achievements, together with acknowledgment and acceptance of one's limitations."[61] I define self-acceptance as accepting your current self-concept without judgment. You look at your strengths and weaknesses, your successes and failures, and you view them as neutrally as possible. You assess your abilities and limitations as objectively as you can, almost in a detached sense, and use your conclusions to inform your actions.

Someone with a self-loathing mind-set might think their failures indicate that they will always fail when they try something new and experience lowered feelings of self-worth and self-esteem as a result. Someone with a self-acceptance mind-set might assess their failures objectively to determine where they could improve in the future and where they already perform well.

Self-acceptance helped me escape the absolutes that contributed to my self-loathing. I grew up in the American South, in the Catholic Church with divorced parents who loved *Star Wars*. Rigid mind-sets about good and evil, right and wrong, and heaven and hell shaped me. My black-and-white thinking[62] also dictated that every story needed a hero and villain. Someone to cheer for. Someone to root against. A heart of gold we love to love and a coldhearted monster we love to hate.

The good guys versus the bad guys.

If you're a bad guy, sometimes the entire world wants to see you burn. Every viewer and character on the good guys' side roots for your ruin on the edge of their seat. They feed on your failure. They thrive on your pain. Understandably—we don't get the satisfaction and closure of justice often in real life. Media and entertainment supplement that for us. That's why movies that pit the

---

61 American Psychological Association. (n.d.). Self-acceptance. In *APA Dictionary of Psychology*. Retrieved April 2023, from https://dictionary.apa.org/self-acceptance.

62 *Black-and-white thinking* refers to polarized thinking or thinking in extremes and absolutes with little to no room for nuance or shades of gray.

good guys against the bad guys and give us a clear victor are so delicious. They offer us a target for our anger. They make us an unspoken promise that the subject of our outrage will get their just deserts. And then, despite any nail-biting complications, they deliver on that promise. The good guys win in the end. Unexpected, tragic, or horrific movie endings that deviate from this formula captivate some audiences, but there's a reason the biggest box-office blockbusters rely on the high of a happy ending: it's the ending most people pay to see. I don't blame them. Those endings comfort and satisfy me, too.

Every piece of media I consumed, the Catholic Church's strict laws about sin, and my parents' good guy–versus–bad guy level of contempt for each other made one thing excruciatingly clear. You want to be a good guy. You do *not* want to be . . .

Dare I even say it?

. . . a *bad* guy.

Whatever you do, be the hero.

Always tell the truth.

Always be kind.

Always be responsible.

Always do the right thing.

Always sacrifice for the greater good.

Always, always, always. Absolutes resounded in every rule. It seemed simple enough. An easy moral compass to follow for audiences, congregations, and kids of divorce of all ages. The complications—for me, at least—occurred when the instructions contradicted themselves.

I should always tell the truth. Got it.

I should also always be kind. Sounds good.

Wait . . . so what exactly should I do when my best friend asks me if I like their truly horrendous portrait they spent three days painting in art class?

The truth would not be kind.

Kindness would not be the truth.

The cursed contradictions! I couldn't find a way to escape without breaking at least one sacred good-guy rule.[63] I wondered if maybe I wasn't as good a good guy as I wanted to be. *Gulp.*

As I got older, the rules further confounded me. I wanted to do the right thing, but complications and contradictions made it ever harder to figure out what the "right" thing was. It seemed like no matter what I did, there would always be at least something a little bit wrong with my choice.

Thinking in absolutes about the world and myself prohibited me from being a good guy. I made too many mistakes. That left me with no other option but to assume I was a bad guy. That combined with my black-and-white thinking contributed heavily to my self-hatred. If one of my achievements didn't reach the highest level of success, it was automatically a failure. If I did something wrong, it's because I was fundamentally a bad person.

Self-acceptance let me look beyond the good-guy, bad-guy mentality and instead see myself as just a guy. An in-between guy. Neither hero nor villain. Just a regular human with regular abilities and limitations, regular strengths and weaknesses, regular failures to learn from and successes to celebrate.

Self-acceptance accommodated me more than the artificial self-love portrayed in the media (constant positive feelings), which kept me stuck in this chicken-and-egg loop where I hated myself for hating myself. I realized I had unrealistic, negative biases

---

63 I lacked the social savvy to maneuver such situations as a kid. As an adult, I've learned through trial by fire that there are ways to escape this maze unscathed. For example, I could have omitted my overall opinion on the portrait and instead shared something specific I liked about it, thereby both telling the truth and considering my friend's feelings. This possibility escaped me when I was stuck in the absolutes of my youth.

against myself. I tried to heal these biases, reason against them, or replace them with a neutral or positive mind-set, and I grew frustrated when I couldn't. I perceived my inability to remove my negative biases as partial confirmation of the biases' validity. I unintentionally reinforced the bias. I hated myself because I hated myself. Trying to force positive feelings about myself when they weren't happening fed this cycle and my self-hatred.

Self-acceptance let me look at my negative biases without judgment or expectation. I sat with my self-hatred, grief, and anger without trying to fix them or wish them away. I just let them exist. They were and are parts of me. Shaming myself for them or trying to rid myself of them only perpetuated my cycles of self-hatred because it reinforced the idea that parts of me are inherently bad. That wasn't, isn't, and never will be true.

I am not inherently good or bad.

Neither are you.

We're human. We experience and express a range of positive and negative emotions. I taught myself how to regulate my big emotions.[64] I realized they're really not that scary.

I started to unpack my trauma. I considered the roots of my

---

64 From the start to the present, that's taken about four years. The first two years consisted mostly of learning awareness. I learned how to identify, name, and physically feel emotions instead of ignoring, suppressing, or intellectualizing them. That was overwhelming within and of itself. I didn't start seeing progress toward being able to efficiently, successfully emotionally regulate beyond a base level of awareness until 2021. Now, in 2024, I can regulate well as long as I'm not overstimulated. Emotional reactions that previously would have rendered me distraught for several days now take me approximately five to ten minutes on average to identify, feel, and release in a safe environment. Sometimes I'll feel something so strongly that I really don't have it in me to regulate. When that happens, I just have to let it happen. I get myself somewhere private to cry, run, break something in a controlled way, etc. My preferred method of emotional release in these instances is sob-screaming into my voice memos in my car. I like to verbally process.

fears of the unknown and perceived losses of control. I slowly worked to reconcile conflicting ideas. Remember, two things can be true at once. No, my traumas and how they molded me into a neurotic, angry person were and are not my fault. Yes, I am responsible for my actions and how I treat others, no matter how traumatized I am. I cannot control or change what happened to me, but I can work on the way I regulate, communicate, and engage in healthy relationships now.

The deepest roots of my self-hatred ran parallel to my trauma. I didn't like who I'd become in response to my trauma, how I treated myself, and how I treated others. I knew I needed to take accountability for my unhealthy behaviors to become a version of myself that I liked, but I couldn't hate myself into healing. Instead, I had to accept the version of myself who existed in that moment. I told her she was enough even with her mistakes. I told her she was worthy of being seen and loved and receiving care. I told her she deserved a chance to live a better life. Self-acceptance made it possible for me to stop seeing myself as the inherent villain.

Self-acceptance also helped me facilitate body acceptance. My body image was negative for most of my life. A combination of generational trauma, the culture of my hometown and country, and my personal traumas motivated me to hide. I wanted to be small. More than anything, I wanted a way to not be seen. To move undetected. I felt safest when I couldn't be found. Being tall, big, and curvy made it hard to hide and made me feel unsafe for a long time, so I hated my body for it. I blamed my body for my constant feelings of unease and distress. If only I weren't so big, maybe I would be safe and happy.

Self-acceptance helped me shift from hating my body to coexisting with it. I applied the same objective framework that I applied to my holistic self-concept to my physical self-concept. I intentionally and actively tuned out all the external forces working against my shift to objectivity, just like I tuned out the extremes about the good guys versus the bad guys. Instead, I turned my attention to people who lived at peace with their bodies to see what I could learn.

I passively studied people who looked like me and seemed to be okay with looking like me. I observed how they spoke about and carried themselves, and how they dressed, cared for, and touched their bodies. I stopped pinching, pulling, and twisting the skin on my stomach, arms, back, and legs while willing it to shrink. I stopped hiding from myself. I stood in front of the mirror, looked at my naked body, and sat with the wide range of emotions that flared until I calmed down enough to start my skin-care routine. I paid attention to how soft, kind, smooth touches made me feel compared to harsh, nitpicking pinches as I applied moisturizers and sunscreen. I watched how my body naturally sat and moved when I stopped contorting it. I forced myself to look at my body without saying anything positive or negative about it. I described what I saw in purely objective terms. No "ugly" or "pretty." No "good" or "bad." Only descriptions of the actual shapes, lines, tones, textures, shadows and highlights that added up to me.

As I simultaneously worked through my unprocessed trauma and practiced physical self-acceptance, I stopped resenting myself for my bigness. I realized what happened to me wasn't my body's fault. I realized my body was just as hurt by my trauma as my being was, but all this time, my body faced that hurt alone while I blamed her for it. I did everything I could to care for my body compassionately. I wasn't always sure how to do that, but I dedicated myself to learning and trying, and that's all my body ever wanted. As I prioritized objectivity and compassion in my relationship with my body alongside general self-acceptance, my self-esteem quietly increased.

Self-esteem is one of the concepts often confused with self-love.

The APA defines self-esteem as "the degree to which the qualities and characteristics contained in one's self-concept are perceived to be positive. [Self-esteem] reflects a person's physical self-image, view of [their] accomplishments and capabilities, and values and perceived success in living up to them, as well as the ways in which others view and respond to that person."[65] In the US, we use the terms *low* and *high* to describe self-esteem. Someone with low self-esteem typically views their psychological and physical characteristics, qualities, and skills negatively. They might describe themselves, their bodies, or their skills as bad, valueless, insignificant, unworthy, undesirable, useless, inferior, or in other negative ways. Someone with high self-esteem generally views their characteristics, qualities, and skills positively. They might describe themselves as good, valuable, useful, important, etc. Having high self-esteem does not make someone arrogant or narcissistic. Arrogance and narcissism are extreme, unhealthy versions of high self-esteem, and self-hatred is an extreme version of low self-esteem.

Healthy, high self-esteem begins with self-acceptance (objectively assessing your self-concept). You determine which of your qualities and characteristics make you proud, happy, confident, etc., and balance those positive feelings about yourself with awareness of your areas for improvement and self-regulation (keeping a record of behavior, assessing that record of behavior, and reinforcing desired behaviors). Thus, self-esteem can increase or decrease. To me, self-esteem is a state of being more than anything else. It's kind of like happiness. You can't force yourself to feel genuine happiness, but you can facilitate happiness by adopting behaviors and mind-sets that bring you stability, fulfillment, inspiration, and peace. Self-esteem works similarly. You

---

65 American Psychological Association. (n.d.). Self-esteem. In *APA Dictionary of Psychology*. Retrieved April 2023, from https://dictionary.apa.org/self-esteem.

can't force yourself to feel good about yourself if you genuinely don't, but you can raise your self-esteem (make it more positive) by working on self-love, self-care, self-focus, self-regulation, and self-acceptance.

Some people believe feigning confidence can increase your self-esteem and combat self-sabotage by positioning you to act how a confident person would instead of acting based on fear. Personally, I prefer self-acceptance over false confidence. Viewing myself exclusively with unfounded positive biases is just as detached from reality as viewing myself with unfair negative biases. Extreme positive biases and delusional confidence also create cognitive dissonance within me that decreases my self-trust when I do, say, or think something that I do not believe a confident, purely positive person would do, say, or think. I would rather have a strong, secure sense of who I truly am and what I can truly do than exist in a fragile state of false confidence that crumbles or creates cognitive dissonance when externally tested.

A realistic evaluation of my self-concept does not limit my potential for growth; it strengthens it. I can be honest with myself about my strengths and limitations and how they interact with my aspirations. Then I can make an informed decision about how much risk I'm comfortable assuming as I work toward my goals. I can still step out of my comfort zone and do things that scare me, but I choose to do so without falsely assuming that my efforts guarantee an externally successful outcome. I push myself to try new things and reward myself for trying regardless of the external outcome. I balance belief in my strengths and my capacity for success with recognition of the factors outside of my control. By doing so, I allow myself to learn and grow in such a way that does not threaten the long-term health of my self-trust and self-esteem even when I fail or make a mistake.

Self-acceptance and self-trust increase my confidence while

still allowing it to fluctuate, which it always will. Confidence is never concrete. Self-love and self-care must be viewed independently from confidence and self-esteem. You deserve love and care no matter what levels of confidence and self-esteem you experience or maintain.

Section V: Self-Worth

Self-worth is another way we assess ourselves. Similar to self-esteem, self-worth is often conflated with self-love despite the definitional and functional differences between the three concepts. The APA defines self-worth as "an individual's evaluation of [themselves] as a valuable, capable human being deserving of respect and consideration. Positive feelings of self-worth tend to be associated with a high degree of self-acceptance and self-esteem."[66] Notably, the external world impacts how we evaluate our value as human beings. Existing in a society that treats you like you lack value or don't deserve equal respect and consideration negatively impacts self-worth, which is why it's so problematic and illogical to treat self-worth, self-esteem, self-love, and self-care like the solutions to every problem that results in negative emotions. Self-love is not the answer to every injustice. Self-care cannot solve structural issues. We'll chat more about the limitations of individual concepts of the self in the next chapter, my dear.

Self-worth sits at the top of the Self-Worth Web. It draws from the foundations of self-esteem and self-acceptance. Self-acceptance and self-esteem rely on nonjudgmental, active awareness of and compassionate, objective engagement with our self-concept. Our self-concept is informed by self-focus,

---

66 American Psychological Association. (n.d.). Self-worth. In *APA Dictionary of Psychology*. Retrieved April 2023, from https://dictionary.apa.org/self-worth.

self-regulation, self-care, and self-love: general and specific ways we consider ourselves and our needs and act based on them or toward our contentment.

I created the Self-Worth Web to escape the commodified, industrialized versions of self-love and self-care that contributed to my self-hatred for years. The concepts and definitions included in the Self-Worth Web affect everyone, but my understanding and explanation of how all the concepts flow together and can be applied is based on my needs and lived experience. You decide the extent to which and ways in which the Self-Worth Web might help you.

WRITING PROMPTS FOR FURTHER REFLECTION

As I mentioned earlier, I like to process verbally. To talk things out. I enjoy journaling, too. Working through my thoughts somewhere physically outside of my brain helps me keep my brain quiet. These writing prompts are designed to help you reflect on and *consider* applying all the concepts and ideas we chatted about in this chapter.[67] You don't have to use all or any of them. You don't have to write your answers. You can talk about these ideas with yourself (perhaps on a voice memo, like me!). You can talk to your friends, family, therapist, priest, or pet about these ideas.

---

67 And I do mean *consider.* I want you to do what feels right for you. If you already know my approach to something won't work for you, awesome! Toss it into the garbage! Light it on fire! You do not have to use or believe anything that doesn't feel right for you, and there is no weird unspoken expectation from me that these things have to be helpful. I am literally your fairy godmother. I'm here for the magical vibes and to see you smile. That's it. Actually, and also for cheese. Humans have good taste in cheese.

You can journal about them. You can think about them on your own. These are tools that are here for you if and when you want them. You do not have to and are not expected to do anything other than that which feels *right* for *you*.

Remember two things as you work through these questions. First, it's okay to be unsure. No one, least of all me, expects you to have all the answers. We're here to work together to think about these things. The important part is the thinking. We celebrate our efforts regardless of the outcome, my dear. Second, there are no right or wrong answers, and you are always allowed to change your mind.

Prompts

1. Look at your response to the writing exercise at the beginning of this chapter. (In case you need a reminder, at the beginning of this chapter I asked you, "When you think of yourself, what first comes to mind?") How do you feel about your response now? Do you think your first thought about yourself reflects your entire self-concept? If so, in what ways? Do you think your first thought about yourself is a conditioned response (whether you or someone else conditioned it)? Why or why not?

2. How do you define love? Is it conditional or unconditional? Have you ever felt, received, and/or given healthy, consistent, vulnerable, reciprocal, safe love (be it familial, romantic, or platonic)? What does love as an action mean to you? In other words, how do you SHOW you love someone? If you could wave your magic

wand and be loved in the healthiest, happiest way for you, what would that love look like in your daily life (again, be it familial, romantic, or platonic)? Do you model this kind of love in your relationship with yourself and/or others?

3. What concepts on the Self-Worth Web interest you most? Why? Which concepts surprised you or were new to you? Does my understanding of these concepts and the interactions between them support or contradict your understanding of them? How?

4. Who has physical or personality traits similar to yours that you like about them but dislike about yourself? This can be someone you know personally or a public figure, celebrity, historical figure, etc. What do you like or appreciate about those traits in that person? Why? Is it possible to shift your perspective on those traits within yourself since you already value them in others?

5. Do you think the Self-Worth Web can help you? How? Why? What parts might you change to better suit your needs?

6. Can you think of any people who modeled the concepts in the Self-Worth Web for or around you? Did anyone teach you about these concepts (intentionally or unintentionally)? What did you learn from them? What behaviors or mind-sets have you internalized from them (whether they're good, bad, or neutral)?

7. What does self-hatred or self-loathing mean to you? How does it feel physically, and what thought patterns do you associate with it? How has it impacted your life thus far? What are its roots (consider both your personal experiences and the broader cultures and environments that shaped you)? What reinforces it?

8. How do you feel when you think about self-care? Do you feel the same way when you practice self-care? Does self-care intimidate you? Do you resist it? If self-care upsets you because it's too draining or complicated, how can you simplify it and make it more accessible for yourself (ex. - using baby wipes if you can't shower, doing your chores while sitting down instead of standing, microwaving a frozen meal instead of cooking, etc.)?

9. What self-care tasks matter most to you? How can you design daily routines based on these tasks that accommodate your lowest resource and energy levels? (The internet has a TON of good advice to help with this! Try looking up self-care or accessibility hacks for people like you. For example, I have ADHD, so I might look up "self-care for ADHD" or "how to make laundry easier ADHD").

10. What does self-love mean to you? How do you understand it, and does this understanding help you or frustrate you?

11. What parts of your self-concept do you struggle to accept? Why? If you had to describe them using only

objective, neutral terms, how would you describe these parts of your self-concept and the reasons they exist?

12. How would you describe your body image? What factors contribute to how you feel about your body? Do ableism, fatphobia, racism, sexism, or other forms of prejudice impact your body image? How? Try to look at your body outside of the lenses of beauty standards and prejudice. How would you objectively describe your body to an artist who's never seen you so that they could draw you?

13. How would you describe your current everyday levels of self-esteem? Are they low or high? When has your self-esteem been low or high at different points in the past, and why—what influenced it? What makes you feel good about yourself and confident now (no matter how fleeting or small the feelings are)?

14. Have you ever intentionally self-regulated or emotionally regulated before? If you have, what strategies work well for you? Why do you think they help? If you haven't, what strategies might help you regulate? What do you need when you feel overwhelmed? Do you need space from other people and a quiet place to calm down? Do you need to talk it out with someone? Do you need physical affection or sensations (like holding something cold) to ground yourself? Do you need to expel your energy via exercise, shaking it out, taking a lap, hitting a punching bag, destroying something (as safely as possible), etc.? Do you need to scream into a voice memo in your car?

15. Are there any parts of yourself (physical or internal) that you are scared to face? What are they? To the extent that you feel safe to do so, can you explain why they scare you?

16. How does your society, community, or culture impact your self-worth? How does your society, community, or culture treat you and people like you? How do you feel about this treatment? Have you ever talked to anyone about this? Would you?

CHAPTER 3

SELF-CARE CAN'T SOLVE EVERYTHING:
The Good, the Bad, and Social Movements and Media

A society's culture, economy, and government define and reinforce what makes a person valuable. If a person does not fit their society's definition of valuable, they are often treated disrespectfully and inconsiderately at individual, communal, and structural levels regardless of their individual self-esteem. With the support of our communities and loved ones, some of us can still maintain high levels of self-esteem even when individuals mistreat us from time to time.[68] However, if we are mistreated, disrespected, discriminated against, or otherwise devalued not only by individuals but also by our local communities and larger societies on a regular basis, our ability to maintain the belief that we are valuable and worthy of respect suffers. No

---

68 This is partially why self-love should not be mutually exclusive with communal and interpersonal love. Humans need lots of love.

matter how resolutely we *want* to believe in our inherent human value, it is difficult to sustain that belief if the world around us denies it.

Individual concepts like self-esteem and self-care can't solve structural and systemic injustices,[69] which impact self-worth. Expecting individuals to completely remove pain and struggle from their lives with self-care reinforces toxic positivity, places the burden of responsibility for reactions to injustice on the shoulders of oppressed individuals instead of the systems that oppress, and makes concepts like self-worth inaccessible for huge portions of the population.

All right. That was a lot of problems I just rattled off. Let's start with toxic positivity.

Toxic positivity forces a positive lens/perspective on everything in life, even genuine challenges and pain. Toxic positivity encourages and expects people to maintain a positive, happy attitude and outlook no matter their circumstances. Toxic positivity can minimize, invalidate, dismiss, discourage, and shame expressions of negative emotions or equate expressions of pain to selfishness or ingratitude. Sometimes people unknowingly engage in toxic positivity because they don't know how to empathize.[70] This is different from someone using toxic positivity to avoid offering someone true support. In either instance, toxic positivity boils down to the simple idea that every experience must be good or

---

69 Though caring for yourself in a society that oppresses you is a radical act.
70 Expressions of pain make some people uncomfortable. Some people don't know how to listen to others talk about suffering and offer empathetic responses because no one did/does that for them. Alternatively, some people feel unprepared to face their own suffering and therefore do not want to engage with subjects that illuminate their pain. I say this to offer potential explanations for behaviors, *not* justifications. Just because you understand why someone does something doesn't mean you must allow them to do it to or around you if it hurts you.

beneficial in some way. Toxic positivity doesn't allow bad things to be bad. That's what makes it toxic.

It's vital to let bad things be bad. Amid abuse and instability, especially when faced with the deaths of loved ones and friends, I didn't want to be happy. I was angry. I wanted to screech at every single person who told me to "look on the bright side," well intended as they may have been. My anger was a natural response to what I perceived as injustice.[71] Why was anyone telling *me* how to *react* to the injustice instead of telling the people or conditions perpetuating the injustice to cut it out?

We cannot truly control anything in life other than our perspectives, and even they can evade our control at times depending on our environment and the information we have at hand. Toxic positivity is an attempt to regain control of perspective, which I understand and respect in theory, but it misses the point in execution. Forcing ourselves to seek out good or feel positive emotions in every situation is ineffective at best and detrimental to the human experience at worst.

Pain serves a purpose. Negative emotions give us just as much actionable information about our identity, our goals, our values, our morals, our boundaries, our self-concept, and the world around us as positive emotions. Anxiety, anger, sorrow, grief, fear, jealousy, and other negative emotions keep us informed. Where toxic positivity fails is by telling us to avoid or repress these emotions. Anger dissipates when I allow myself to feel and release it in safe ways. Fury festers when I attempt to push it down, numb it, ignore it, or suppress it.

---

71 I phrased this sentence this way to be gracious. I believe with every fiber of my being that specific things that happened to me are definitionally unjust, but I know the truth is subjective and relative when it comes to abstract concepts like justice (not *legality,* but specifically justice).

Instead of following the toxic positivity model of avoiding/ suppressing negative emotions and forcing ourselves to look for silver linings in every situation, I prefer to practice self-acceptance and emotional regulation. I'm a human being living in an unpredictable, unprecedented world that teeters on the brink of global disaster each day. My feelings in a vacuum are valid, whatever they may be, but it is my job to react to my feelings responsibly. We feel, process, and release emotions in safe, healthy ways that don't endanger ourselves or others. If we aren't able to do this, we work on emotional regulation and self-regulation until we can. Just like self-love is not constant positive feelings about yourself, true positivity and perspective allow us to feel the full range of human emotions. We are allowed to react to injustice with anger, which leads me to my next point about collective structural and systemic issues.

The wellness, weight loss, and diet industries pump billions of dollars into conning us. They convince us our bodies are "bad" and sell us snake-oil solutions "guaranteed" to fix us. Over time, the same industries strategically change the definition of "bad" based on market and consumer trends to increase their sales. It doesn't matter if your body was "good" or "bad" *last* year. All that matters is their newest definition of "good" and whether you fit it. You never win when you run their race. You aren't supposed to. You're supposed to keep running. Keep buying new products forever just so you can barely escape the label "bad body" that looms over your shoulder and trails ever closer behind you.

You and your body are not bad, my dear.[72] The industries intentionally undermining your self-esteem and polluting your self-concept to increase sales are bad. Not you. I'm so sorry if

---

72 Unless you mean bad as in the good kind of bad, in which case you're bad to the bone.

these industries scammed you out of your resources before, whether you lost money, time, or both. They got me, too. I'm most retroactively enraged by the time an MLM (multilevel marketing) representative tried to sell me "magic slimming wraps" over an Instagram direct message when I was fifteen. I nearly paid eighty dollars (USD) for what I later realized was literally just cling wrap and lotion. I can't even recall all the ridiculous, useless products I drooled over and nearly bought because I thought they'd finally give me a "good" body in my teens and early twenties.

Good and bad are moral concepts. Bodies are not moral. Bodies vary in functionality, ability, appearance, size, and shape, but such variances are neither morally significant nor indicators of worth. Health, ability, productivity, and desirability are not universally accessible and should not be treated like precursors for respect, consideration, and visibility. A body is not immoral or bad if it lacks a limb. A body is not moral or good if it fits current beauty standards. Bodies can have disabilities. Bodies can have chronic illnesses or be unhealthy. The same body can be called strong or weak, beautiful or ugly, big or small, healthy or unhealthy, and endless other relative descriptors, but no matter what, that body is not inherently morally bad.

As the vessel through which we live our lives, our bodies intrinsically impact our self-concepts. However significant and impactful, a body is still just a body. A living, physical organism. The actions we take with our bodies can be moral, but our bodies themselves and the parts and systems that operate within them exist outside of and separately from morality.

Like self-love narratives, conversations about good and bad bodies often lead to miscommunications. In Part II, Chapter 2, we discussed the disadvantages of (and my personal frustra-tions with) using *self-love* as a blanket term for all concepts of the self and positive feelings about the self. Similar frustrations and disadvantages exist with describing bodies as bad and good. In the preface of this book, I conceded that life would be quickly convoluted if we explicitly defined the context and exact meaning of every word we use every time we used it.[73] Sometimes we say one thing, and someone hears or interprets something else.

Some people don't use the words *good* and *bad* in a moral sense when describing their bodies. Sometimes people mean *good* as in desirable. Sometimes people use *bad* to signify suffering, like saying your stomach feels bad when it hurts. These amoral uses of *bad* and *good* remain subjective and impermanent. Your body is not inherently bad because you experience pain. Every human being to ever live has experienced pain at some point. Desire relies on subjective individual and collective values. The collective beauty standards and individual personal preferences that determine desirability change. Someone may find your physical features desirable, and someone else may not. There is not one, dominant, objective beauty standard. Our bodies are not inherently, objectively desirable.

Whether or not a body is good or bad takes on another level of significance when we talk about functionality and identity. Marginalized bodies are subjected to discrimination and sometimes treated like they are inherently bad by the people and systems that oppress them. This is one of the primary reasons why we can't tell people to "just love themselves more" or work on their self-worth and self-esteem when we talk about self-hatred. Existing in a body that not only lacks equal rights and opportunities but also

---

73 Even I don't want to do that all the time, as much as I love a definitional debate. Sometimes I just want to make my puns, disappear back into my room, and wait to hear my roommates' muffled laughter and booing from the other room. If I define every word in the setup for my pun, I lose my comedic timing, and that just won't do, my dear.

makes you a target for attack leads to complex feelings of resentment and self-hatred that I cannot even begin to fully fathom and am not remotely qualified to speak on as a white, cisgender woman.

My experience living as a fat person on the smaller end of the plus-size spectrum profoundly impacted my self-hatred,[74] and I barely faced the tip of the iceberg of structural fatphobia *and* still benefited from thin privilege. I didn't even know I had thin privilege until I learned more about the body-positivity movement. That within and of itself—learning I had privilege instead of knowing I lacked it based on how the world treats me—is an example of privilege. I never encountered the majority of the access issues that impact fat folks. Even at my smallest and least healthy, I didn't consider myself thin, but thin privilege isn't about your self-image.[75] Size privileges and discrimination are access issues. Yes, I wear plus sizes. Yes, some doctors have assumed I eat poorly and don't exercise without even asking me about my lifestyle. Yes, no matter how my weight fluctuates, I still consider myself big. But I've never been fired from a job or rejected as a job applicant because of my size.[76] Doctors do not outright refuse to treat me because of my size. I don't get harassed by strangers on the street about my weight. I can find clothing that fits in most stores. Before, I took all those things for granted because I never realized not everyone gets access to the

---

74 So did (and still does, at times) living with ADHD, PTSD, and other conditions, as addressed in Chapter 2.

75 From my understanding of it, self-image is part of the conversation about size-based privileges, but it is not the focus. Positive self-image is easier to access as a thin person in an actively fatphobic society. That doesn't mean thin people don't or can't struggle with self-image and body-image. Low self-esteem and self-hatred can affect anyone. However, people in thinner bodies don't face the same systemic, structural, and even social issues as fat people in the US, which is what the concept of thin privilege explains.

76 Weight is not a federally protected characteristic in the US at the time of writing, meaning employers can use weight as a reason to fire or not hire someone (unless their state laws prohibit it).

reality I experience living at my size. People living in bodies larger than mine don't often get such privileges.

Self-esteem and self-care cannot solve these and other structural issues because they are individual concepts. Self-esteem can't fix legislation. Self-care can't erase bigotry and biases. Self-love can't advocate for social and political equality, but people and movements can and do.

The fat liberation and fat acceptance movements formed in the US in the late 1960's and early 1970's created the foundations for what many now call the body-positivity movement. Organizations such as the National Association to Advance Fat Acceptance (NAAFA) and the Fat Underground advocated for equal rights and treatment for fat folks and denounced the diet industry and the sexist, racist, ableist, and fatphobic beauty standards and capitalistic norms it promotes decades before the dawn of the internet age. [77] When the body-positivity movement born out of fat activism started to gain mainstream traction in the media and online, companies and people adopted some of the movement's language and ideals without advocating for its intended purpose: equality for marginalized bodies.

As social media rose in popularity, users across platforms—often led by Black women, LGBTQ advocates, and fat visibility activists—collectively pushed back against the beauty standards curated by diet culture and the so-called wellness industry in the West. Conversations about the reality and extent of image editing grew louder and louder until mainstream media took notice. Regular people outside the entertainment and fashion industries turned to social media to create more realistic expectations of what unedited bodies look like in everyday life. At the

---

77 "NAAFA's Origin Story & Fat Activism History," NAAFA, accessed October 26, 2023, https://naafa.org/history.

same time, many people misused language and ideas from the body-positivity movement. The phrase *body positivity* became synonymous with positive feelings about your body and distanced from its parent movements and original radical intention, similar to what happened with the oversimplification of self-love and commodification of self-care. Social media movements sprang up in response to this co-opted idea of body positivity. Not everyone wanted to (or felt they could) feel positive about their body. Thus, the body-neutrality and body-acceptance movements were popularized. These movements help many people find frameworks to improve their relationships with their bodies, but, like self-esteem, they focus on the needs of the individual, not the collective.

Concepts and movements that focus on the individual serve important purposes, but they can't and don't solve structural issues. You cannot love yourself out of poverty and unmet needs. You cannot love yourself out of racial, gender, disability-based, or size-based discrimination. We cannot answer outrage over injustice with shallow and dismissive toxic positivity. How can we expect marginalized people to heal without acknowledging and working to abolish the injustices that contribute to their self-hatred and providing equitable assistance to help facilitate self-care, self-acceptance, self-esteem, and self-worth?

Truthfully, I am one woman. I point the finger at the problems that perplex me and work to find solutions and fight for change when and how I can, but I cannot solve these problems alone, especially at the structural level. I don't have all the answers to life's big questions. If I did, I'd wave my magic wand and share them with you in a heartbeat. Unfortunately, I can't do that, so I'll give you the next best thing I've got in Chapter 4: my ultimate, magnum opus bulleted list of life advice, the Fairy Godmother's Growth Guide.

THE FAIRY GODMOTHER'S GROWTH GUIDE

A t last, we've made it! The end of the book. Pat yourself on the back. If you skipped ahead to this chapter, pat yourself on the back anyway. I'm proud of you for making it to this day in your life.[78]

Let's take a trip down magical memory lane and revisit what we've learned. We defined self-love and synthesized the Self-Worth Web. We identified factors that can impact self-care and differentiated sustainable self-care routines from singular acts of self-care. We reviewed self-concept, explored self-focus and self-regulation, and distinguished true self-acceptance and secure self-esteem from fleeting emotional highs and lows. We discussed morality, toxic positivity, and injustice in reference to self-worth. We've journeyed far from where we began, but now . . . where do we go?

---

78 And cheers to many more days, my dear!

More specifically, where do *you* go?

I'm not sure where I'll go as Marisa McGrady, but as your fairy godmother, as THE AUTHOR—the omniscient, magical narrator behind the curtain—I'll remain right here within these pages long after you leave.

As for you, I have a few suggestions. The final decision is yours, as always. This is your life. I like lists, so I compiled my suggestions into a list for you. Here:

Where You Can Go from Here

1. To bed. How late is it where you are? Do you have school or work tomorrow? Don't make me materialize in your home, point at the nearest clock, raise my eyebrows, and wave my magic wand disapprovingly at you.

2. To the kitchen. Have you eaten? Go get a snack. Drink some water. Hydrate.

3. To—

—hmm? I'm sorry, is this not what you had in mind?

Oh! You wanted to know *what* you can do, not *where* you can go. My apologies. There's that silly little tendency of mine to take things literally again. Let's make a new list.[79]

Before we dive into the new list, let me caution you. I don't recommend trying to do everything on this list simultaneously or

---

79 Isn't this fun? I love this kind of inside-joke, footnote dynamic between writer and reader. Hopefully you do, too. I can't imagine how annoyed you must be at this point in the book if you don't . . . oh, well. No point ruminating on it now.

immediately, especially if you haven't tried these things before. Self-focus and self-regulation can be confusing and draining. Learning how to regulate takes trial and error. Sometimes you think you need space when you really need to be held. Sometimes you think you need to vent when you really need to be alone with your thoughts. If you lived in unsafe environments where you weren't allowed to feel your feelings or outwardly express emotion, you'll need time to adjust as you explore these new concepts and practice these new skills.

We crave familiarity, sometimes even when the familiar is painful. Our unconscious conditioning can draw us toward circumstances that aren't good for us just because they're familiar. We may feel hesitant about newer, better circumstances just because they're unfamiliar. As you learn and grow, you might not enthusiastically say, "Yes! I want that!" to a good circumstance right away. You might feel unsure about it, suspicious of it, or bored by it. Safety and stability can unnerve people who find comfort in chaos.

As we heal, we learn how to tell healthy excitement, anticipation, and fear apart. We learn to separate stability from boredom. We slowly learn how to listen to ourselves. If something isn't stressful or scary, our bodies might not boom "YES!" or "NO!" at us right away. Sometimes a yes comes in a quiet curiosity, a wondering if hope is worth entertaining. Sometimes growth whispers instead of screaming. Don't ignore something just because it starts as a maybe. Listen to the information within you, even if you aren't sure how to act on it yet. Ponder the shades of gray instead of forcing yourself into extremes. It doesn't have to be an immediate, intense "YES!" to be good for you.

Ease into self-care tasks. Behaviors take time to evolve into routines, and you won't know which self-care tasks you want to turn into routines until you try them. You don't have to implement twenty new daily tasks all at once. You probably shouldn't. Pick a few new things to try at a time. Don't overwhelm yourself. Decide which self-care tasks most benefit you, and then practice them until they become routines. Remember to create your routines based on your *lowest* resource and ability levels. This will help keep self-care accessible even when you're low on money, time, or energy, and do not let capitalism, classism, or anything/anyone else make you feel bad about how you practice self-care for a single second! Frozen meals, fast food, and prepackaged snacks are still FOOD. Eating them is better than not eating at all. Doing chores while sitting instead of standing still gets the chores done. Physically resting your body even if you can't fall asleep is better than not resting at all. Wiping yourself off with a wet towel or baby wipe is still cleaning yourself even if it isn't a shower or bath. Sitting outside for a few minutes, even if you just sit there because you're too tired to do anything else, still exposes you to fresh air and sunlight. You deserve care on your best and worst days, and there is NOTHING WRONG with making accommodations to keep care accessible.

Forgive yourself when, not if, you forget about certain self-care tasks or lack the energy for even the most accessible versions of them. Your progress does not reset if you forget or skip part of your self-care routines. Self-love and self-care are not all or nothing. They are about learning, trying, and growing at your own pace.

Approaching self-care like this allows room for emotional reactions, too. Practicing regular self-care can feel pointless, selfish, and overwhelming at first. Those feelings can linger for days, months, and years. They can dissolve right away. They can change. They can fade and then randomly show back up when you least expect it. It depends on your current self-concept and the factors that contribute to it: your cultural and socioeconomic background, your familial and personal history, and your access to resources (including time). You are not bad at self-care just because you aren't sure how to personalize it to your needs and resources yet. You are not bad at self-care just because it feels foreign and unnecessary sometimes (and keep in mind that "sometimes" can last for *years*).

You are learning. You are practicing and using the process of elimination to figure out what helps you and what doesn't. You've got a big list of ideas, behaviors, mind-sets, tasks, and environments to test. Give yourself time and compassion. You deserve it.

I started learning about self-care in 2018. It's taken me five years to feel comfortable saying I understand concepts of the self now, and *I am still learning.* Every day, I learn more about myself and my needs. Every day, the state of my being and my definition of contentment change. The primary and most important ways I love myself are allowing myself to progress, regress, stagnate, grow, change, take breaks, and rest without judgment. Structural and systemic issues exist that contribute to and complicate self-hatred. Negative emotions are part of the human experience. Practicing self-love and self-care is not about achieving a perfect, permanent state of positive feelings. It's about creating circumstances in our lives that allow us to feel safe and content to be who we are.

Please be patient with yourself. Pace yourself. You're figuring all this out as you simultaneously live your life. Life doesn't pause to let you learn. It requires you to learn on the job. Circumstances and people change with complete disregard for your wishes or readiness. That's HARD. It's okay to take this one step at a time.

You're actively living the human experience as yourself for the very first time. Even people with upbringings, cultures, interests, ability levels, resources, and traits nearly identical to yours do not know exactly what it's like to be you. By being you, you're doing something new. Something that's never been done before.

By deciding to *love and care* for you, you are doing many new things. Allow yourself to practice and learn.

And now! Without further ado, here are my imparting suggestions for you, my dearest fairy godchild.

My magical masterpiece . . .

My magnum opus . . .

My most whimsical, wise wishes . . .

BEHOLD!!!!

A guide for life, presented and formatted as a bulleted list:

The Fairy Godmother's Growth Guide

Choose self-love. Self-love isn't a feeling. Self-love is choosing to be aware of your being and interested in your contentment. Pay attention to your needs, wants, desires, and general satisfaction. Are your needs satisfied? Is life satisfying right now? Has it ever been satisfying? Take interest in your well-being even if you can't take action to address it. If you aren't sure how to do this, check out Chapter 2, Section I for further guidance.

Practice regular self-care. Self-care isn't just singular. It isn't something you save for a rainy day. It doesn't require a spending spree. Self-care is acting for your being and toward your contentment. Self-care is fulfilling a set of repeating personal care tasks to meet your basic needs. Start by identifying the daily self-care tasks you want to complete (like eating, hydrating, etc.). Try to assemble these tasks into a list, and store that list somewhere outside your brain. Make a physical or digital copy. When you externalize the list, you don't have to rely solely on your memory to accurately recall the tasks on the list or the steps and tools necessary to complete them. If you struggle with memory and executive functioning skills (like me), try placing physical copies of your list around the house in the places where you complete your self-care tasks (the bathroom, the kitchen, your bedroom, etc.). I do this to remind me to complete certain self-care tasks when I am in specific environments (for example, seeing my list in the bathroom reminds me to wash my face if I haven't showered that day, seeing my list in the kitchen reminds me to eat, etc.).

Make self-care sustainable and accessible. Don't overwhelm or overextend yourself with self-care. Start slow. Add one or two new personal care tasks to your routines at a time. Building routines requires consistency and time. Build your self-care routines around your <u>lowest</u> resource levels, not your <u>highest</u>, to allow flexibility for natural fluctuations in your available resources (your time, money, and energy and ability levels). For example, there's a note on my daily self-care list that reminds me not to let more than four days pass without at least a short shower. It specifies that I don't have to take a long shower or wash my hair or do a multistep skin-care routine if I don't have the energy. I can just take a short, five-minutes-or-under shower. Soap up, rinse off, get out. This flexibility helps me stay consistently clean even when my mental health declines or I get overwhelmed by work.

Examples of daily self-care tasks: Eat multiple times a day; sleep for a minimum of seven hours in each twenty-four-hour period; drink the number of ounces of water your body requires/your doctor suggests daily at the very least;

brush your teeth twice a day; clean your face, hair, and body a few times a week (you determine which frequency best meets your needs given your current resources); detangle your hair; move your body at any intensity level for a few consecutive minutes (determine the type of movement and duration based on your needs, interests, and ability levels— I personally love going on walks); spend time away from your phone, computer, and TV to rest your eyes, even if it's only for a few minutes.

Practice self-focus. Pay attention to your emotions, thoughts, wants, and needs. Notice what triggers your first, conditioned thoughts, and ask yourself why. Observe how your wants and needs impact your daily life. Do you fulfill your needs? What about your wants? Do you ignore them or overindulge? Try not to compare yourself to others. There is no exact, objective truth that fits every single person. Get curious about your emotions without judging yourself for them. Do you feel emotions often? Are you unsure whether you feel things or not? What emotions do you feel the most frequently? What emotions do you rarely feel? When you feel an emotion, how long does it seem to last? How do your emotions physically feel in your body? If you need help figuring out how or where your emotions might physically show up in your body, go back to the questions in the writing exercise at the beginning of Chapter 2 for examples.

Practice self-regulation. Keep track of your behaviors and emotions. Evaluate them. Do you have any patterns or repetitive behaviors? What internal and external behaviors do you engage in every day? (I define internal behaviors as behaviors that mostly occur in your mind, like thinking or imagining. External behaviors are behaviors that you usually take with your physical body, like moving, eating, or talking). How do you respond to your emotions? Are there any emotions you're scared to feel or avoid feeling? Are there any emotions you want to feel but you aren't sure if you ever have? Do you act based on your emotions? Which emotions do you act on? Do you react immediately when emotionally overwhelmed or do you take time (even if it's just a few minutes) to process before you respond? Reward yourself for behavioral patterns you want to reinforce. Be honest with yourself about behavioral patterns you want to discontinue or change. What do you want to change about them, and why? How can or will you attempt to change them?

Build self-trust. Give yourself manageable tasks. Set incremental goals. Each time you complete a goal or task, no matter how small you or others may think it is, take a moment to be proud of yourself. Remind yourself that you said you'd do this thing and acknowledge that you followed through on what you said you'd do. You kept your word, and the thing is done. Remember, it takes time to trust new people. You can't demand that you trust yourself without demonstrating that you deserve your trust. Start with goals and tasks that are easy to achieve to build a solid foundation of self-trust, and slowly increase the size, risk, or complexity of the goals and tasks as you see fit. Don't overextend yourself, but don't be afraid to take risks, either. This is one of those times where the instructions kind of contradict each other because we have to balance opposing ideals. It's frustrating, I know, but I also know you can do it. I believe in you.

Practice self-acceptance. Objectively assess your self-concept. This is easier to achieve when you're in a relatively stable, balanced emotional state. It's hard to be objective about a perceived failure or success when you're still riding its emotional highs and lows. Give yourself time to regulate, and then take an objective inventory of yourself. What are your skills and abilities? What are your limitations and areas for improvement? Remember, the current answers to these questions are not concrete. Your self-concept grows, flows, and evolves as you do. Nothing is ever permanent or set in stone.

Practice physical self-acceptance/body acceptance. Try looking at, describing, and thinking about your body objectively and neutrally. Avoid assigning value, morality, or desirability to your body as you describe it. Focus on the literal shapes and features of your body. Stand, sit, or lie in front of a mirror and look at yourself. Try not to shrink yourself, make yourself look bigger, hide behind your hair or clothes, or twist yourself into specific poses. Simply let yourself exist in as relaxed a state as you can and observe what you see. Do your best to sit with and see yourself for at least a few minutes without turning away. If you aren't used to seeing yourself like this or looking at yourself in general, please only do this exercise somewhere safe for you to feel, express, and process any emotions that arise.

Reinforce positive feelings of self-esteem and self-worth. Celebrate your progress and success. Remember that you are valuable and deserving of consideration and respect even when others don't treat you fairly. Seek out communities that accept and celebrate you for who you are. You deserve love and companionship. Reward yourself for your efforts to incentivize yourself to keep trying. You are doing a good job.

Engage mindfully on- and off-line. Avoid communities, narratives, and content that present opinions as facts. Remember that everyone is at least somewhat biased by their own lived experience, including me and you. Watch out for misinformation. It never hurts to double-check something that feels off. Seek out communities, content, and narratives that inspire, support, uplift, educate, and entertain you. Read, watch, and listen to new materials. Know that not every person, interest, movement, space, hobby, and community you encounter and engage with will be a good fit for you forever. Be okay with letting go when it's time. Be okay with letting in the new. You can change. You can stay the same. Don't let anyone force you to do or be something you do not want to do or be.

Above all else, my dear, *live*. You discover what works best for you by living each day. You can't spend your entire life thinking, strategizing, and planning. It's impossible to know what we would truly do in certain situations until we're in them. You might never find the missing pieces to your theories' puzzles until you stand eye to eye with reality's obstacles, advantages, and consequences: the good, bad, and unknown.

Act on your ideas, desires, needs, wants, dreams, and fears. Make a mess. Make mistakes. Learn from them. Try again.

Celebrate your victories, no matter how big or small. Honor your efforts regardless of the outcomes.

Make peace with the contradictions. They're annoying but unavoidable. They aren't designed specifically to hurt or spite you.

They aren't a cosmic or karmic punishment. They aren't traps or tricks. They're just a part of life. You don't have to like them, but life gets easier if you can coexist with them.

Choose progress over perfection. Remember, progress is often nonlinear, and you are always free to start over. There is no shame in standing back up after you get knocked down, no matter what or who knocked you down, including yourself. Rest. Recover. Get back up when you're ready. The world will still be here waiting to embrace you again every time, and so will I. There is nowhere you could go and nothing you could do that would make me stop loving you. Wherever you go, whatever you do, you will always have a home here with me.

I am in awe of you.

I am so proud of you.

I love you unconditionally.

Go out into the world and do the most magical thing you can do:

Be *you*.

ACKNOWLEDGMENTS

Thank you to the Viva Editions and Start Publishing teams, especially Jarred Weisfeld and Ashley Calvano, for the opportunity to bring this book to fruition and for their patience and support. I literally couldn't have done it without you.

Thank you to every person who's requested or suggested a poem, shared their story in my comments section, encouraged others in our community, and allowed me to be their fairy godmother. Thank you for making magic with me.

Thank you to my family and friends for loving and supporting me throughout this process, especially Mike, Lejani, Jensine, Hugh, Lee, Meredith, Chandler, the Sisneys, and the McGevnas.

Jenny, across all the universe, throughout space and time, there is neither muse nor pen capable of creating a combination of words that could convey the full force of my gratitude to and for you. Since I am thusly bound, I'll settle for "thanks, Mom."

Thank you for every sacrifice, every hug, every screaming match, every birthday book, every phone call, every therapy session, every sliced banana with cinnamon sugar, and your countless other efforts to give my future a fighting chance amid everything working against it. You are the only reason I can even fathom unconditional love. There is nowhere you can go and nothing you could do that would make me stop loving you.